This book Belongs to:

_____

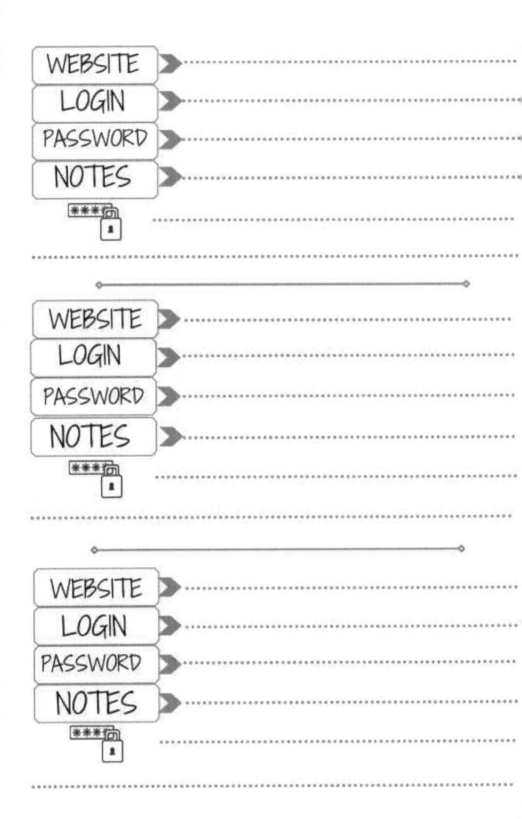

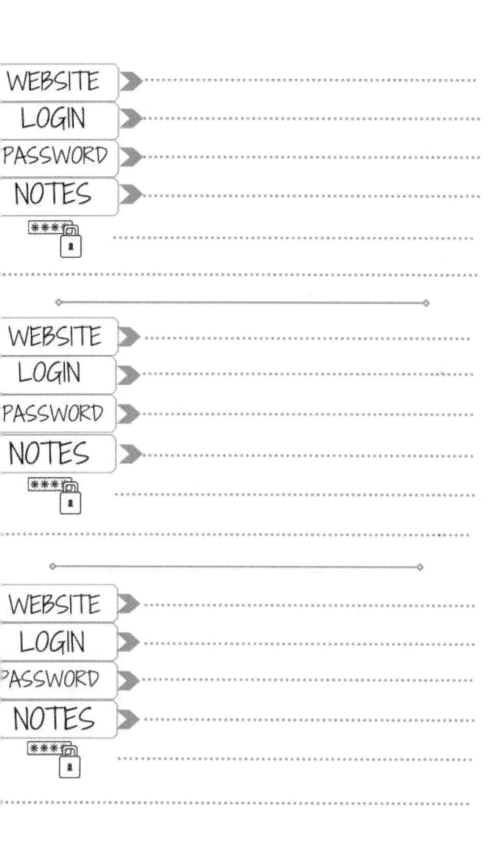

WEBSITE

LOGIN

PASSWORD

NOTES

WEBSITE

LOGIN

PASSWORD

NOTES

WEBSITE

LOGIN

PASSWORD

NOTES

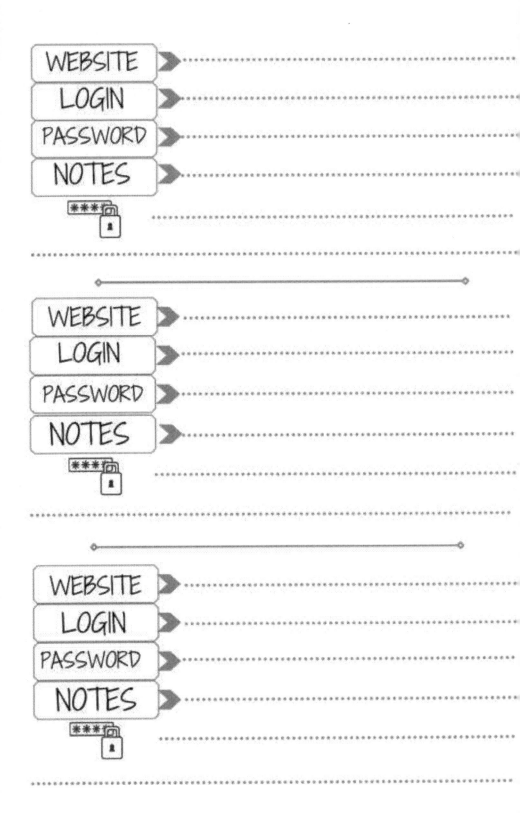

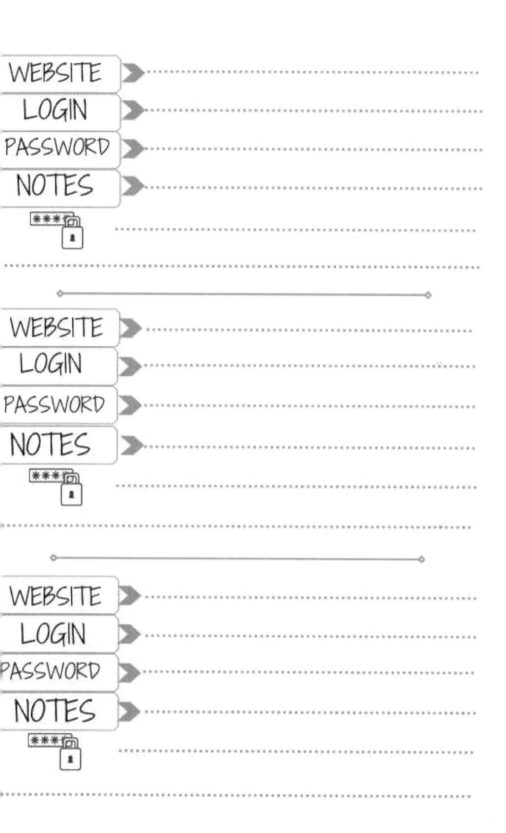

WEBSITE

LOGIN

PASSWORD

NOTES

WEBSITE

LOGIN

PASSWORD

NOTES

WEBSITE

LOGIN

PASSWORD

NOTES

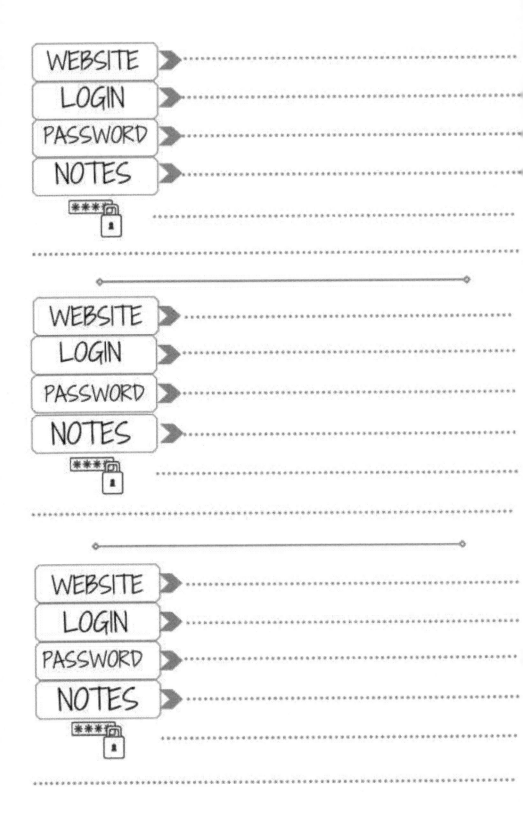

WEBSITE ⯈ ....

LOGIN ⯈ ....

PASSWORD ⯈ ....

NOTES ⯈ ....

....

....

○————————————————————————————————○

WEBSITE ⯈ ....

LOGIN ⯈ ....

PASSWORD ⯈ ....

NOTES ⯈ ....

....

....

○————————————————————————————————○

WEBSITE ⯈ ....

LOGIN ⯈ ....

PASSWORD ⯈ ....

NOTES ⯈ ....

....

....

WEBSITE ....

LOGIN ....

PASSWORD ....

NOTES ....

....

....

WEBSITE ....

LOGIN ....

PASSWORD ....

NOTES ....

....

....

WEBSITE ....

LOGIN ....

PASSWORD ....

NOTES ....

....

....

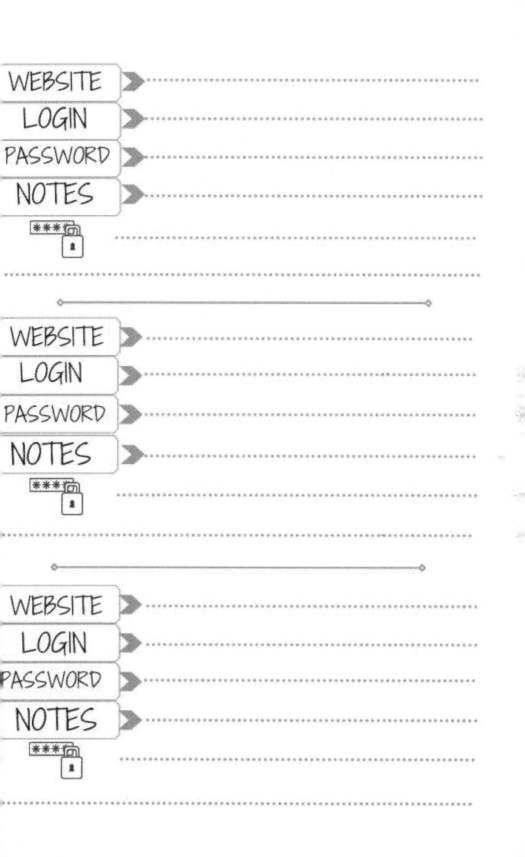

WEBSITE

LOGIN

PASSWORD

NOTES

WEBSITE

LOGIN

PASSWORD

NOTES

WEBSITE

LOGIN

PASSWORD

NOTES

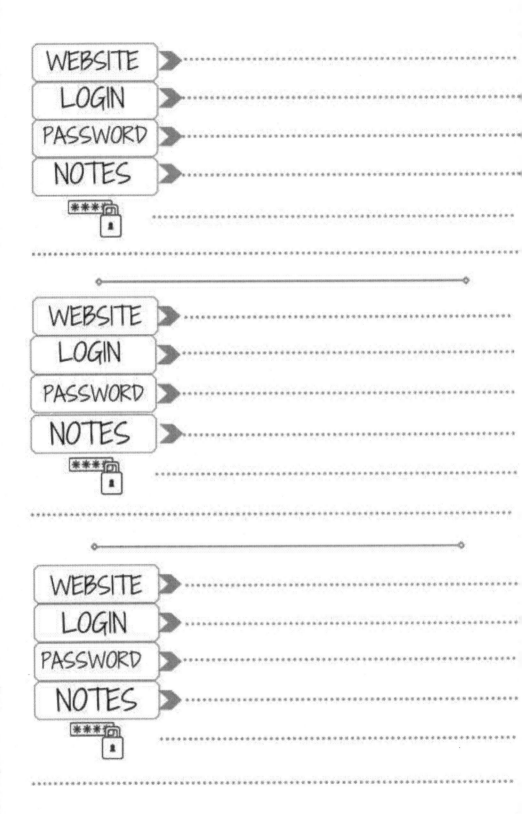

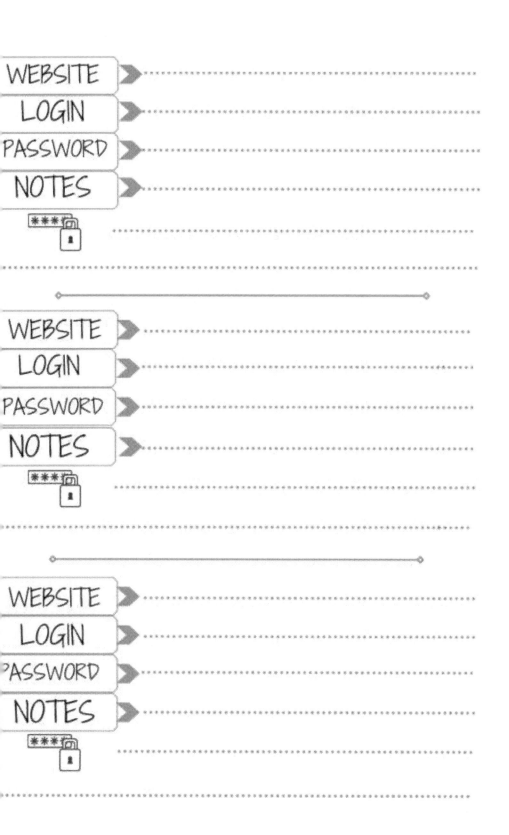

WEBSITE

LOGIN

PASSWORD

NOTES

WEBSITE

LOGIN

PASSWORD

NOTES

WEBSITE

LOGIN

PASSWORD

NOTES

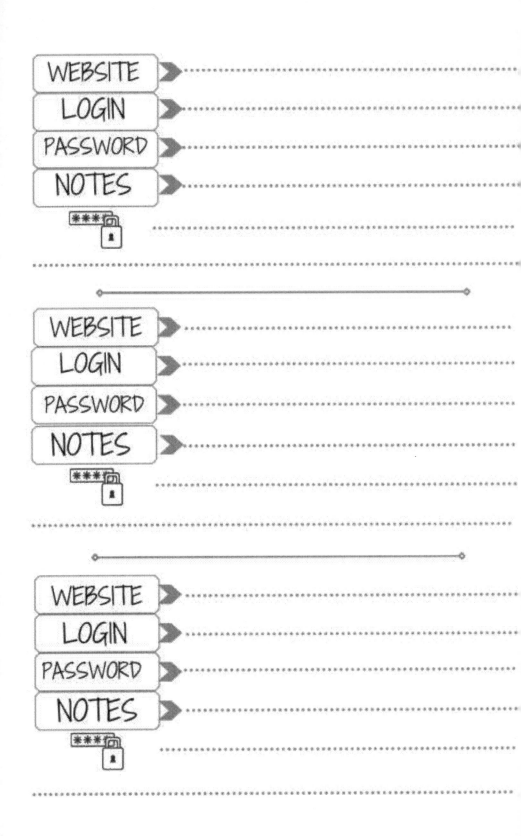

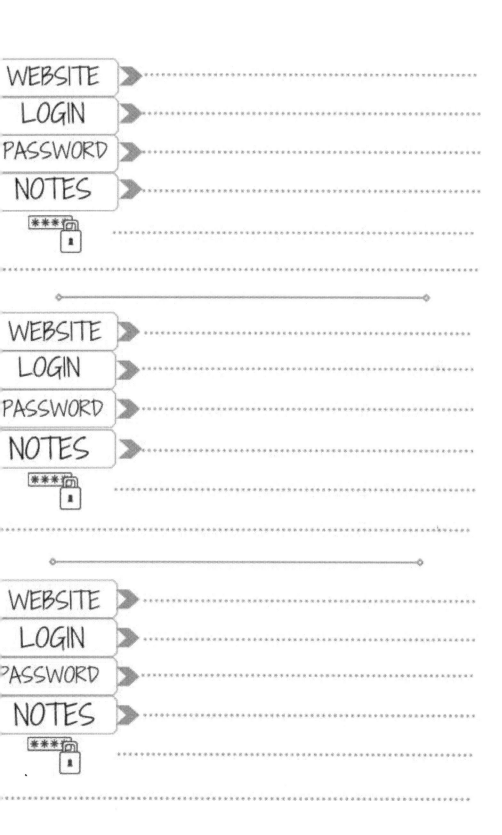

WEBSITE

LOGIN

PASSWORD

NOTES

WEBSITE

LOGIN

PASSWORD

NOTES

WEBSITE

LOGIN

PASSWORD

NOTES

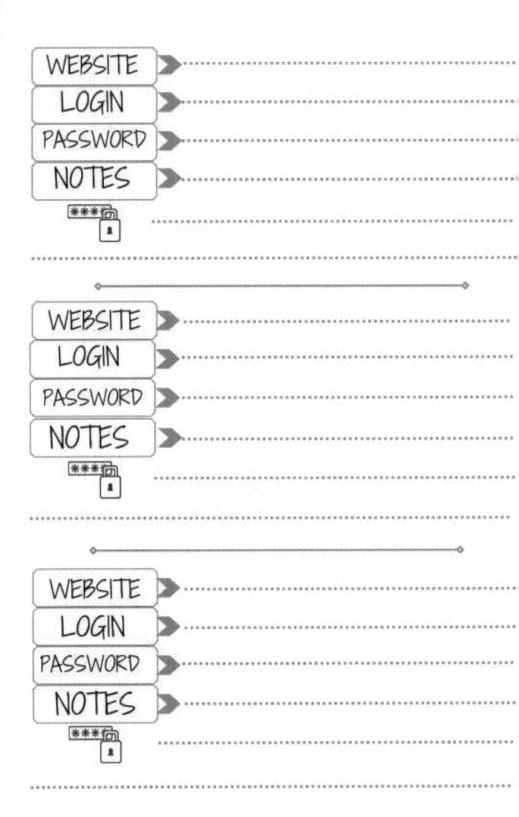

WEBSITE ....

LOGIN ....

PASSWORD ....

NOTES ....

....

WEBSITE ....

LOGIN ....

PASSWORD ....

NOTES ....

....

WEBSITE ....

LOGIN ....

PASSWORD ....

NOTES ....

....

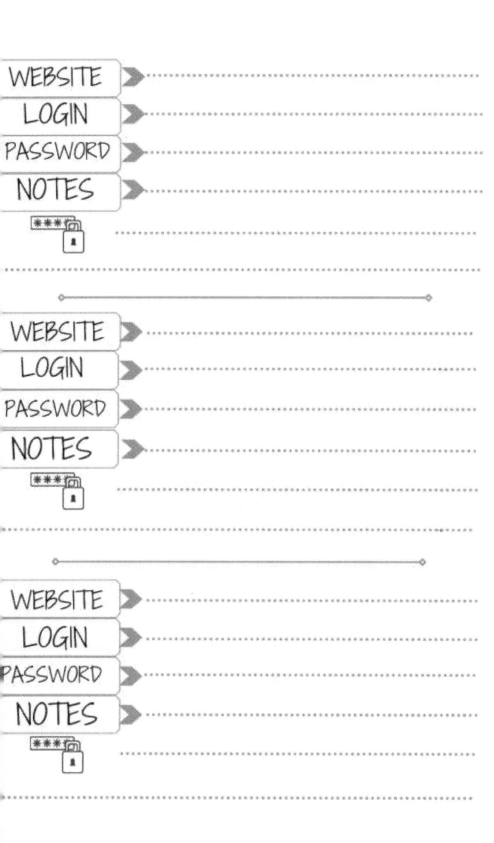

WEBSITE
LOGIN
PASSWORD
NOTES

WEBSITE
LOGIN
PASSWORD
NOTES

WEBSITE
LOGIN
PASSWORD
NOTES

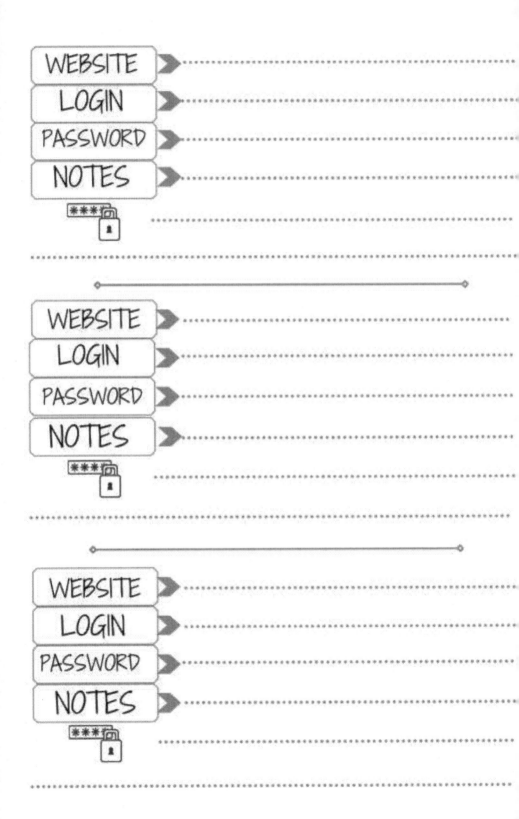

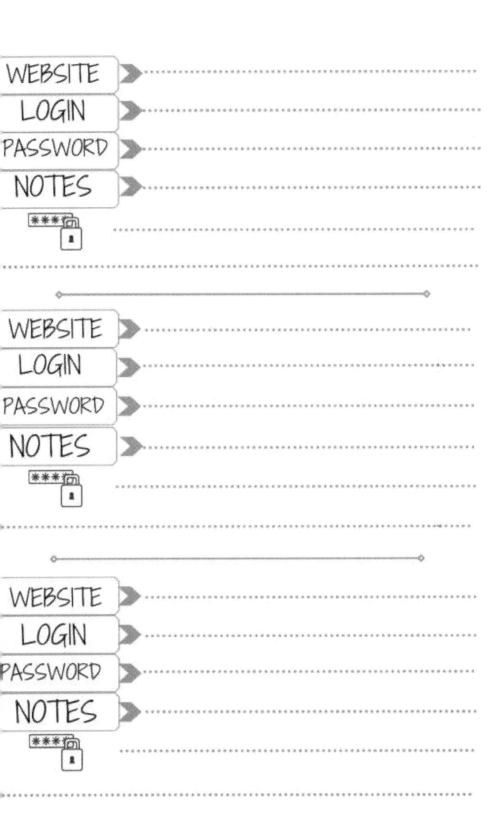

WEBSITE ....

LOGIN ....

PASSWORD ....

NOTES ....

....

....

WEBSITE ....

LOGIN ....

PASSWORD ....

NOTES ....

....

....

WEBSITE ....

LOGIN ....

PASSWORD ....

NOTES ....

....

....

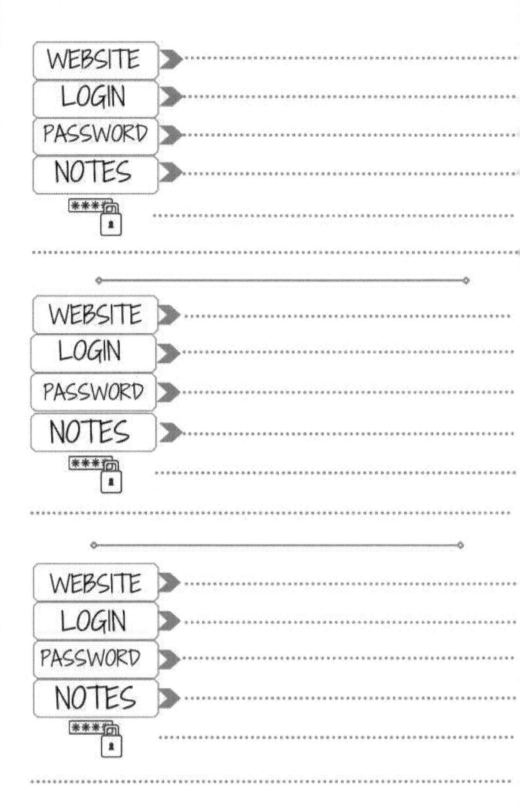

WEBSITE

LOGIN

PASSWORD

NOTES

WEBSITE

LOGIN

PASSWORD

NOTES

WEBSITE

LOGIN

PASSWORD

NOTES

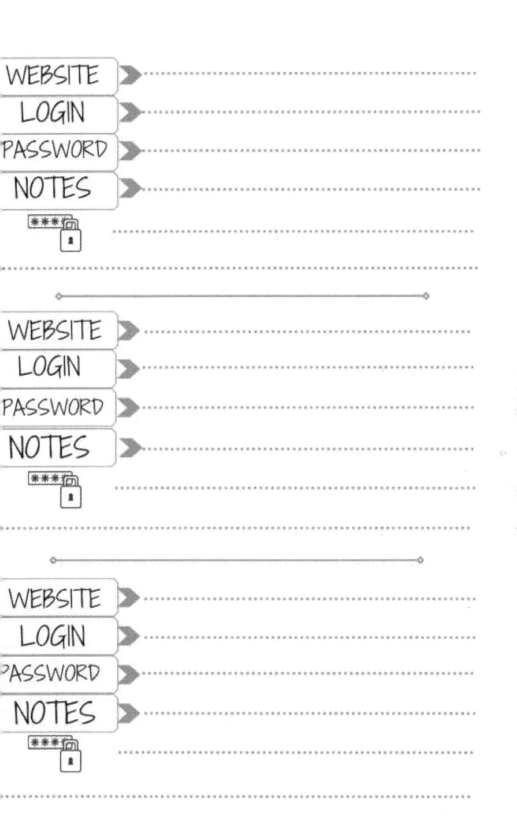

WEBSITE

LOGIN

PASSWORD

NOTES

WEBSITE

LOGIN

PASSWORD

NOTES

WEBSITE

LOGIN

PASSWORD

NOTES

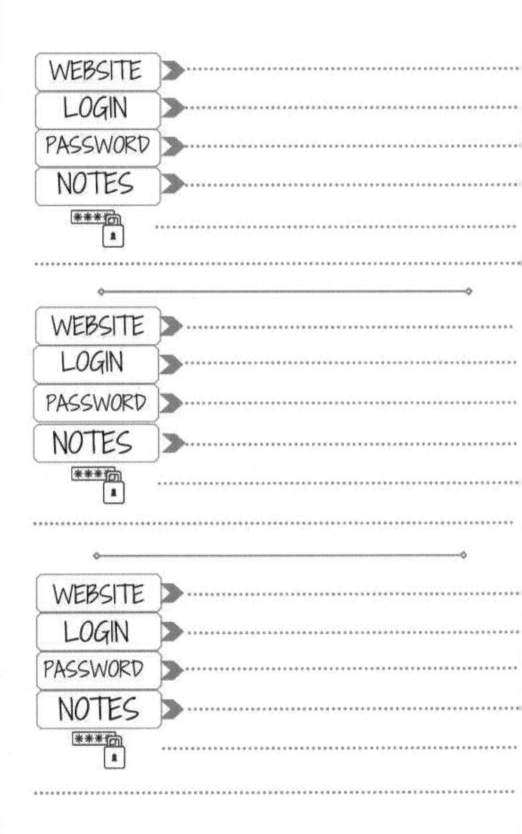

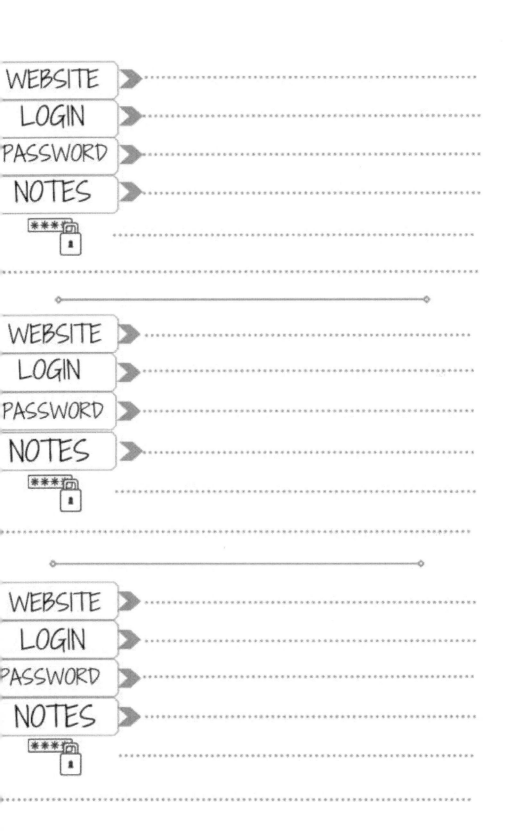

WEBSITE

LOGIN

PASSWORD

NOTES

WEBSITE

LOGIN

PASSWORD

NOTES

WEBSITE

LOGIN

PASSWORD

NOTES

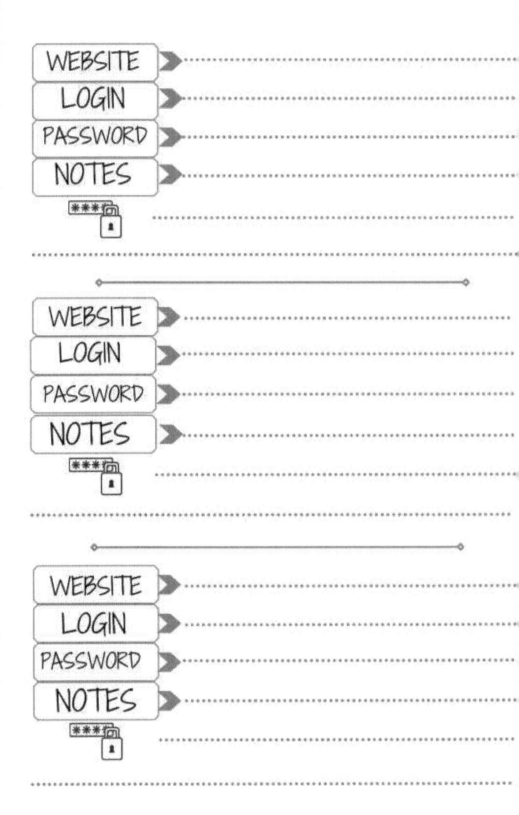

WEBSITE
LOGIN
PASSWORD
NOTES

WEBSITE
LOGIN
PASSWORD
NOTES

WEBSITE
LOGIN
PASSWORD
NOTES

WEBSITE ....

LOGIN ....

PASSWORD ....

NOTES ....

....

....

WEBSITE ....

LOGIN ....

PASSWORD ....

NOTES ....

....

....

WEBSITE ....

LOGIN ....

PASSWORD ....

NOTES ....

....

....

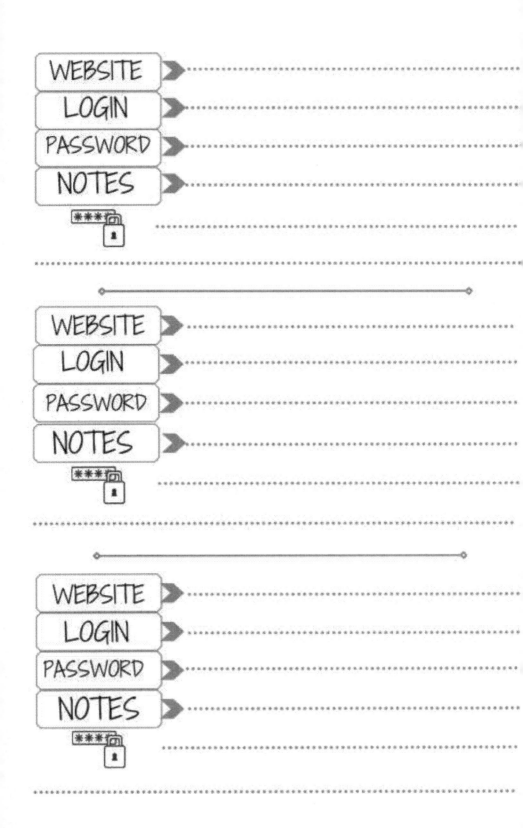

WEBSITE

LOGIN

PASSWORD

NOTES

WEBSITE

LOGIN

PASSWORD

NOTES

WEBSITE

LOGIN

PASSWORD

NOTES

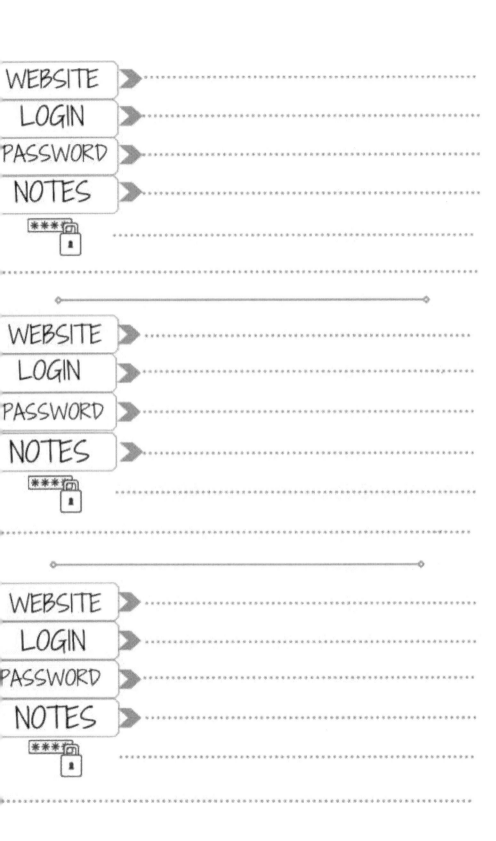

WEBSITE

LOGIN

PASSWORD

NOTES

WEBSITE

LOGIN

PASSWORD

NOTES

WEBSITE

LOGIN

PASSWORD

NOTES

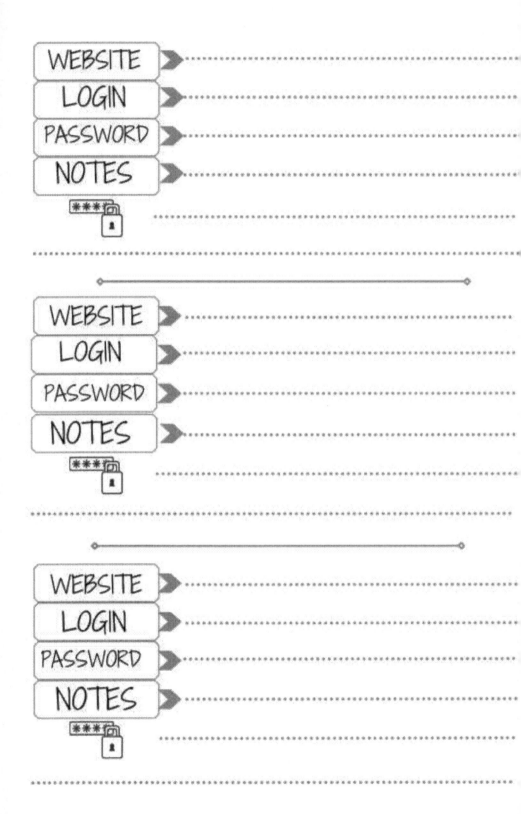

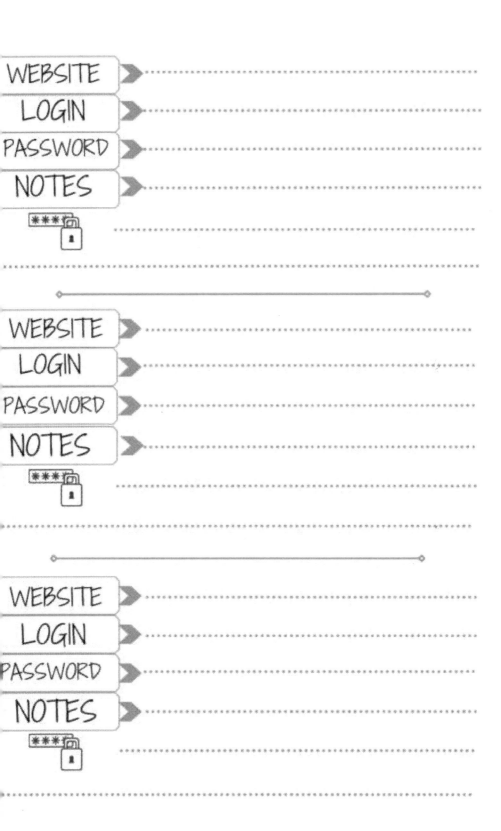

WEBSITE

LOGIN

PASSWORD

NOTES

WEBSITE

LOGIN

PASSWORD

NOTES

WEBSITE

LOGIN

PASSWORD

NOTES

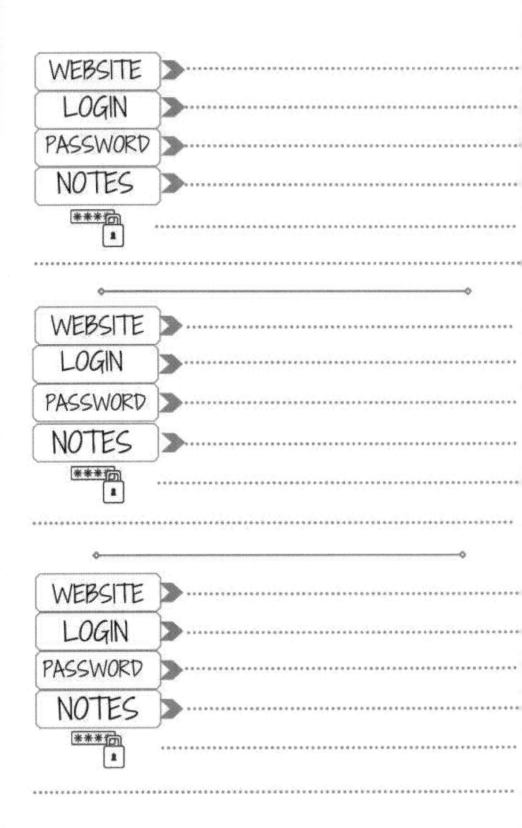

WEBSITE ....

LOGIN ....

PASSWORD ....

NOTES ....

....

....

WEBSITE ....

LOGIN ....

PASSWORD ....

NOTES ....

....

....

WEBSITE ....

LOGIN ....

PASSWORD ....

NOTES ....

....

....

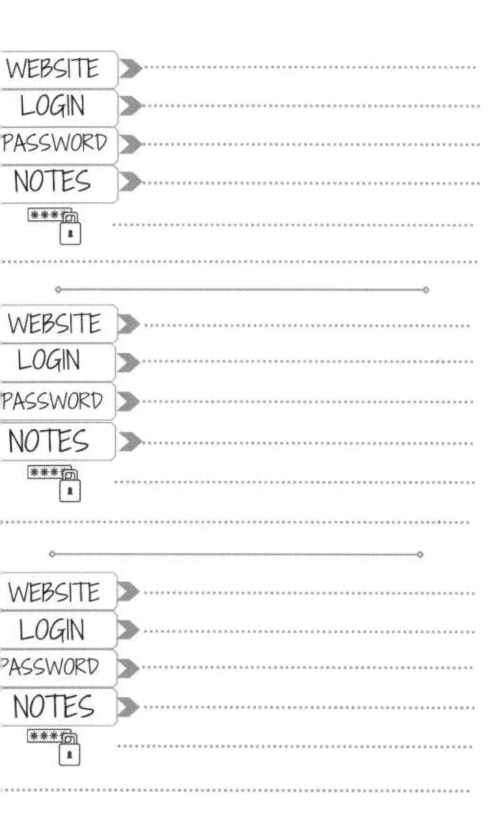

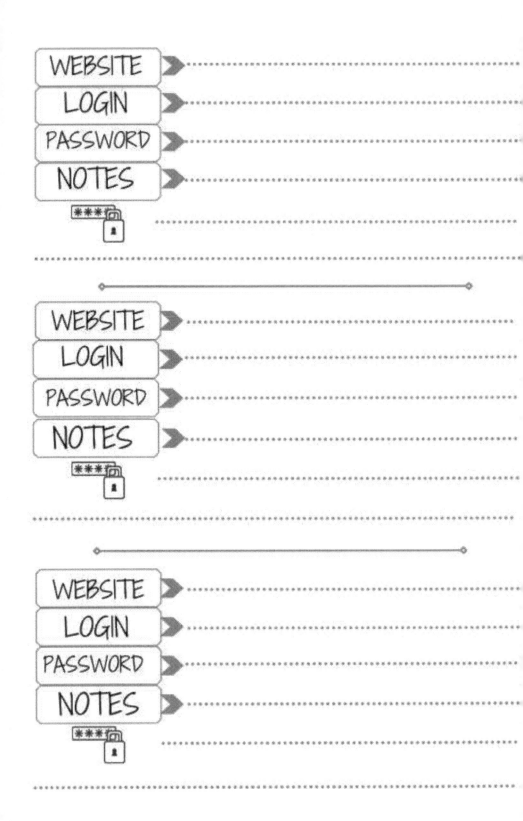

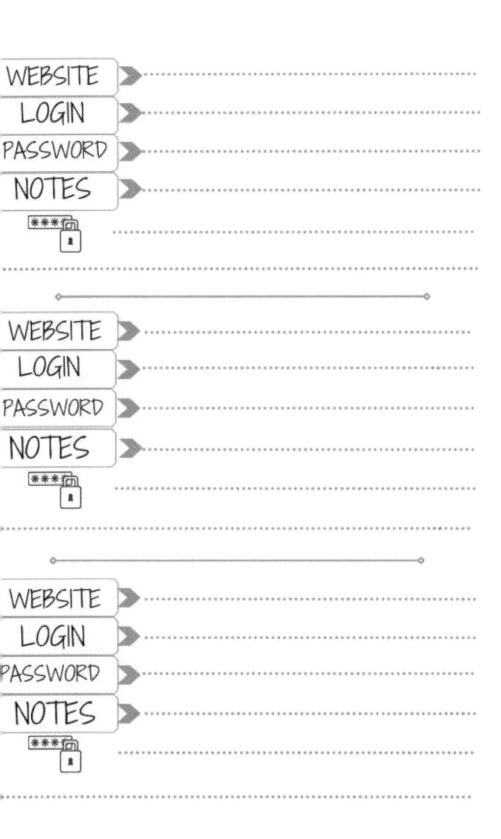

WEBSITE

LOGIN

PASSWORD

NOTES

WEBSITE

LOGIN

PASSWORD

NOTES

WEBSITE

LOGIN

PASSWORD

NOTES

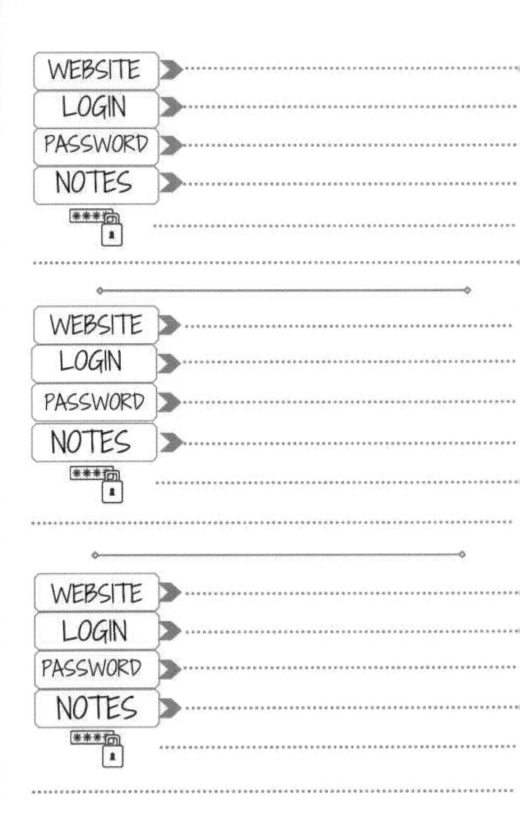

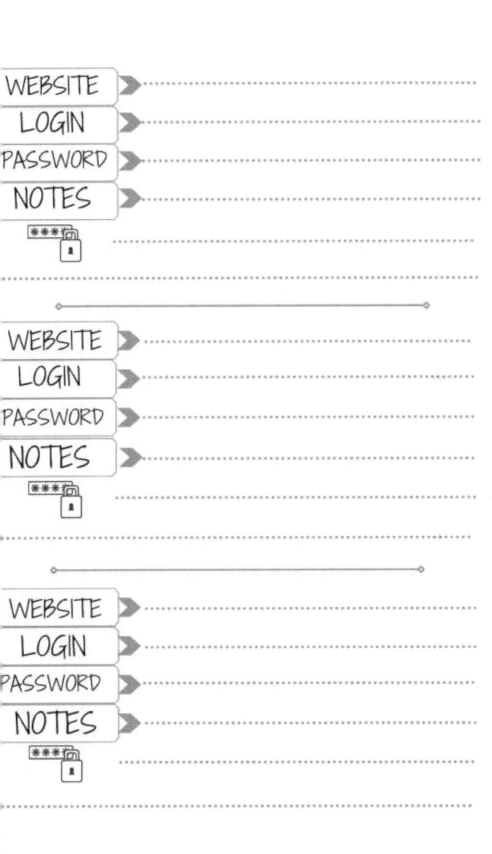

WEBSITE ....

LOGIN ....

PASSWORD ....

NOTES ....

....

WEBSITE ....

LOGIN ....

PASSWORD ....

NOTES ....

....

WEBSITE ....

LOGIN ....

PASSWORD ....

NOTES ....

....

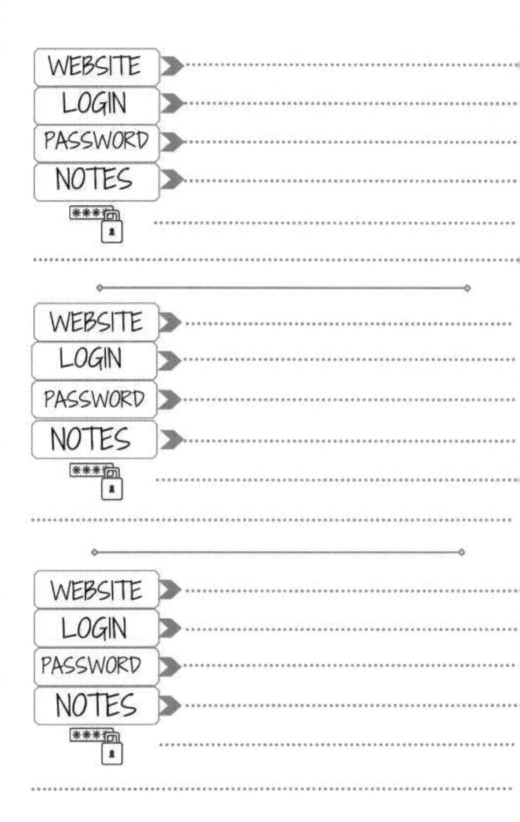

WEBSITE

LOGIN

PASSWORD

NOTES

WEBSITE

LOGIN

PASSWORD

NOTES

WEBSITE

LOGIN

PASSWORD

NOTES

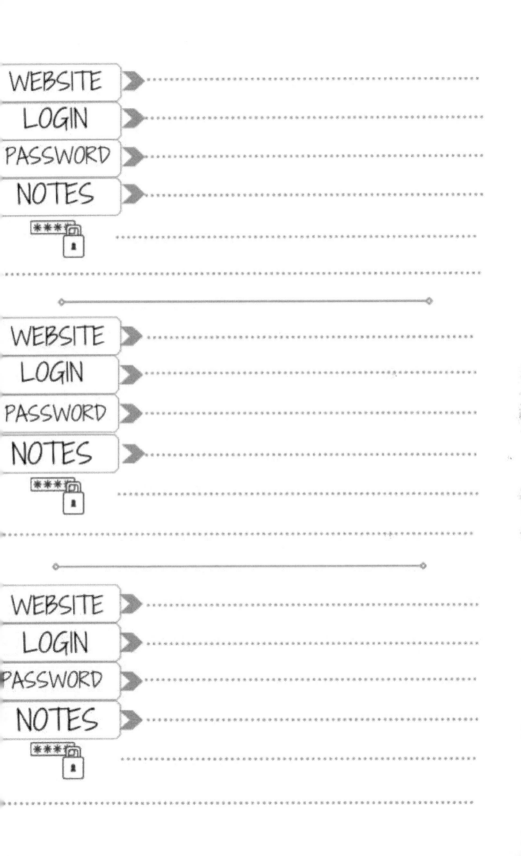

WEBSITE

LOGIN

PASSWORD

NOTES

WEBSITE

LOGIN

PASSWORD

NOTES

WEBSITE

LOGIN

PASSWORD

NOTES

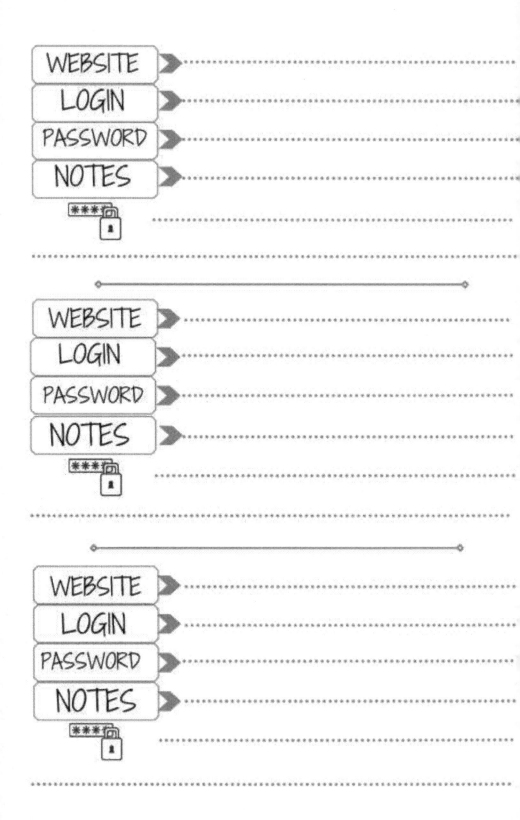

WEBSITE ....

LOGIN ....

PASSWORD ....

NOTES ....

....

....

WEBSITE ....

LOGIN ....

PASSWORD ....

NOTES ....

....

....

WEBSITE ....

LOGIN ....

PASSWORD ....

NOTES ....

....

....

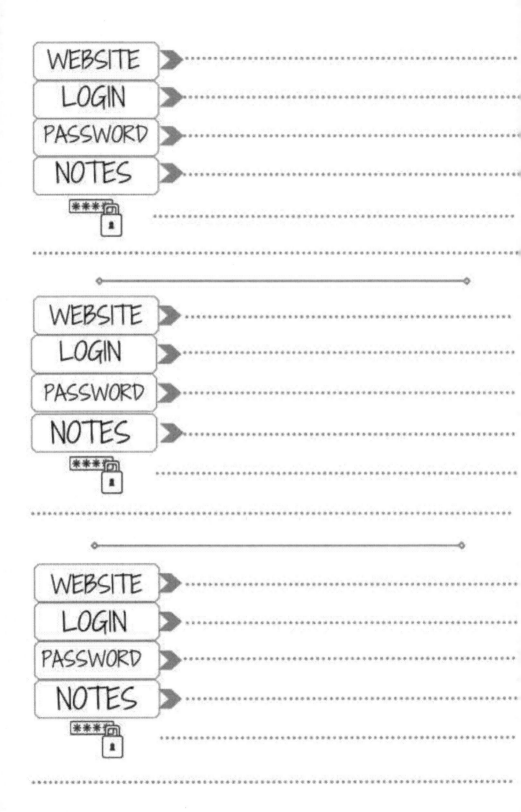

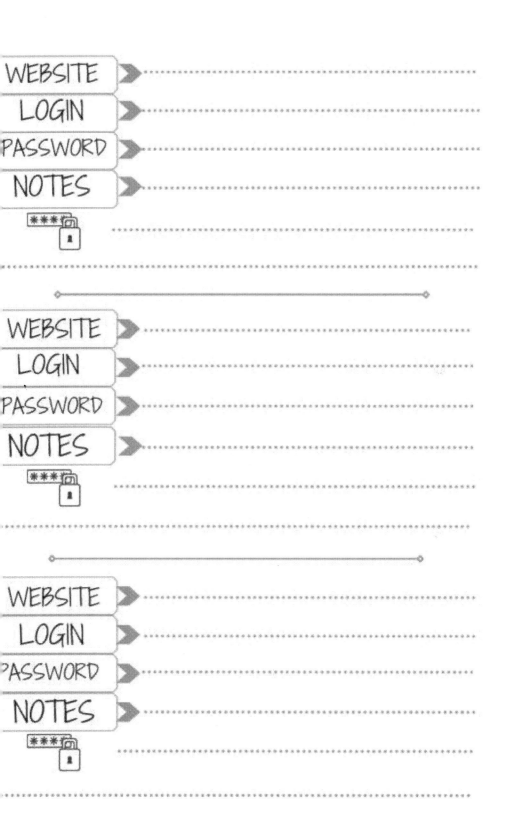

WEBSITE ....

LOGIN ....

PASSWORD ....

NOTES ....

....

WEBSITE ....

LOGIN ....

PASSWORD ....

NOTES ....

....

WEBSITE ....

LOGIN ....

PASSWORD ....

NOTES ....

....

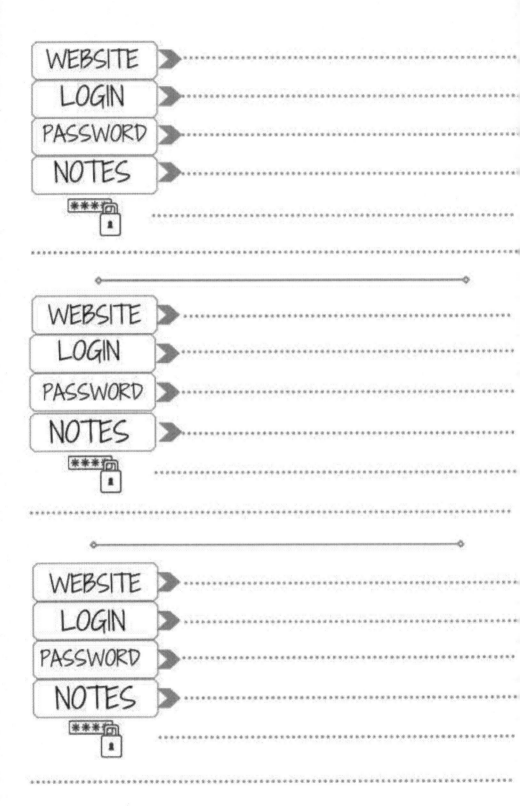

WEBSITE

LOGIN

PASSWORD

NOTES

WEBSITE

LOGIN

PASSWORD

NOTES

WEBSITE

LOGIN

PASSWORD

NOTES

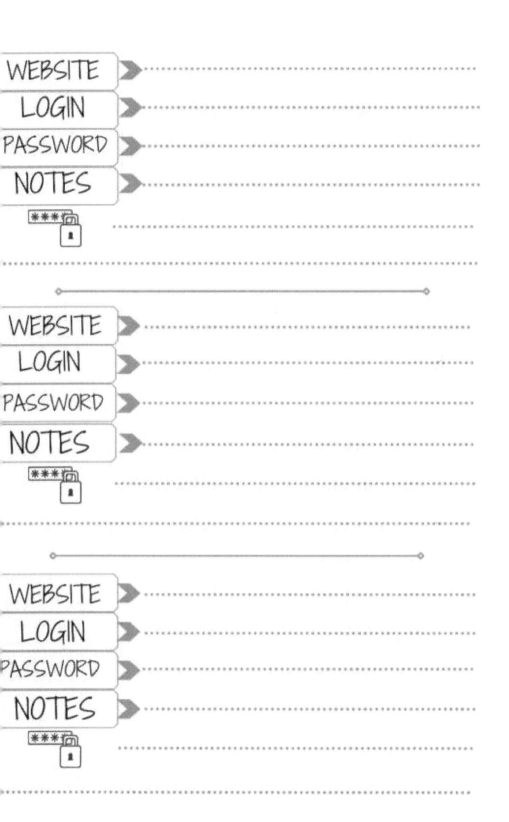

WEBSITE

LOGIN

PASSWORD

NOTES

WEBSITE

LOGIN

PASSWORD

NOTES

WEBSITE

LOGIN

PASSWORD

NOTES

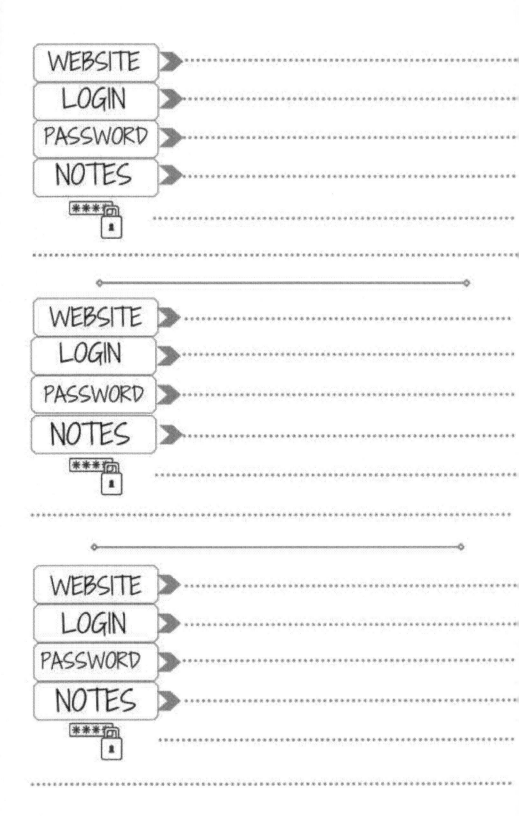

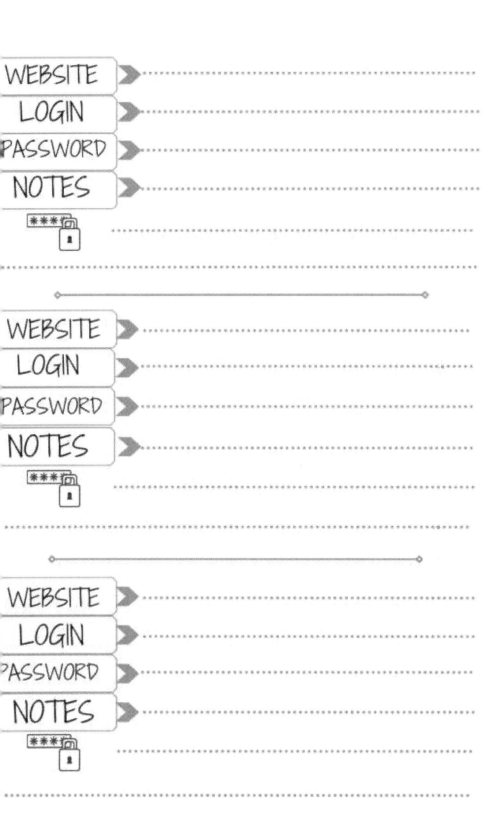

WEBSITE

LOGIN

PASSWORD

NOTES

WEBSITE

LOGIN

PASSWORD

NOTES

WEBSITE

LOGIN

PASSWORD

NOTES

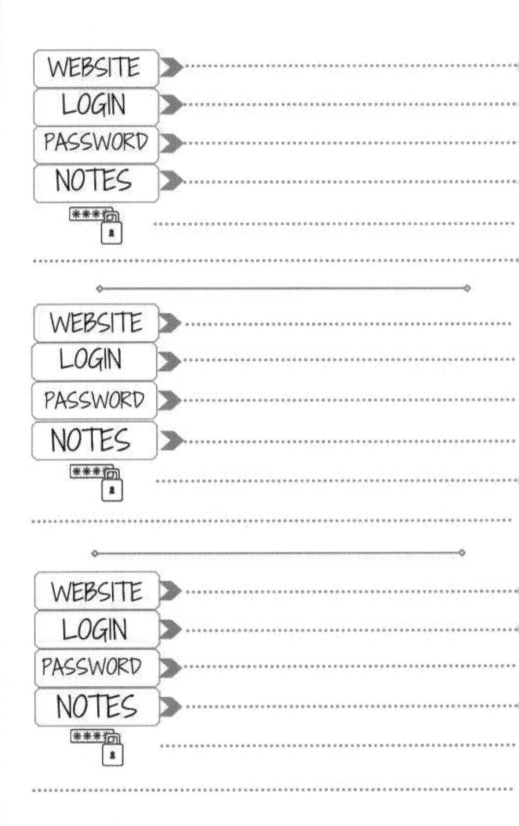

WEBSITE
LOGIN
PASSWORD
NOTES

WEBSITE
LOGIN
PASSWORD
NOTES

WEBSITE
LOGIN
PASSWORD
NOTES

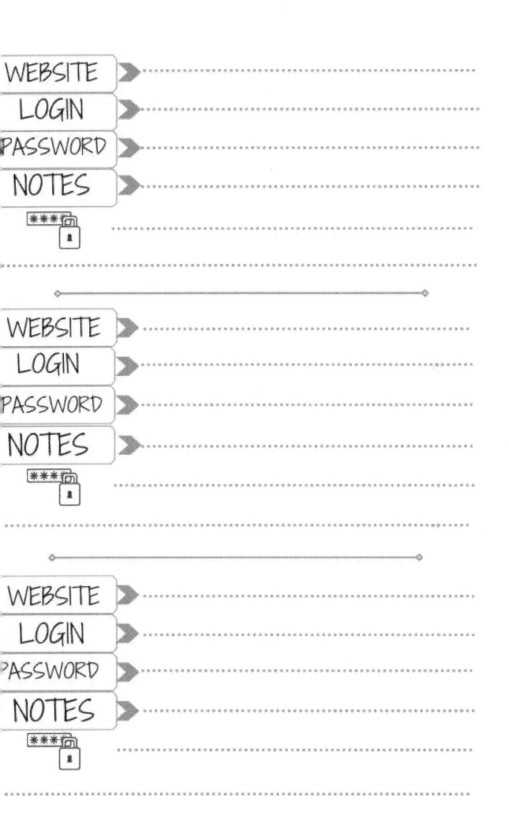

WEBSITE

LOGIN

PASSWORD

NOTES

WEBSITE

LOGIN

PASSWORD

NOTES

WEBSITE

LOGIN

PASSWORD

NOTES

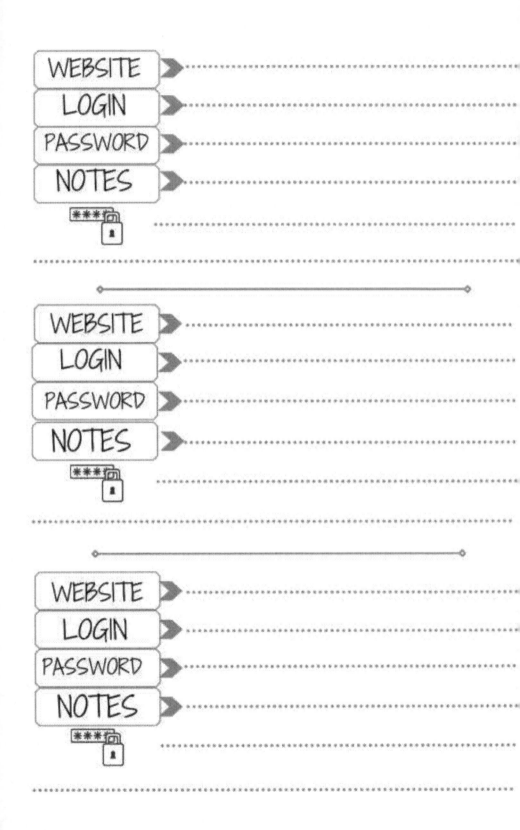

WEBSITE

LOGIN

PASSWORD

NOTES

WEBSITE

LOGIN

PASSWORD

NOTES

WEBSITE

LOGIN

PASSWORD

NOTES

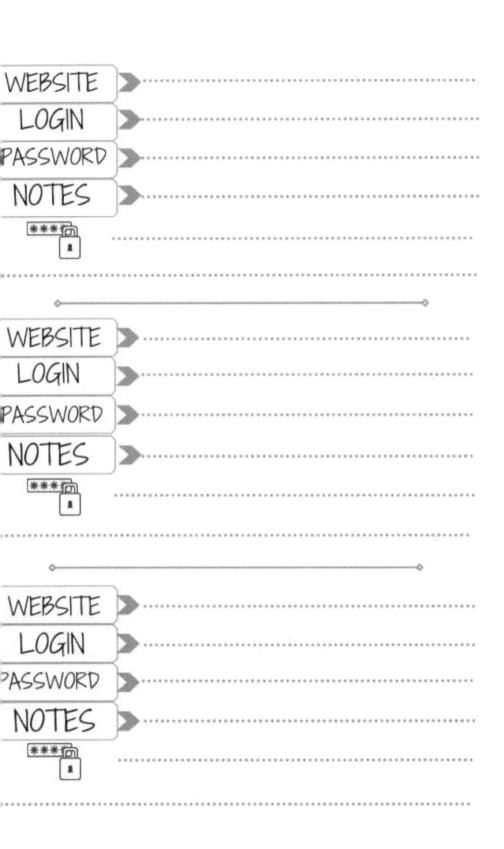

WEBSITE ....

LOGIN ....

PASSWORD ....

NOTES ....

....

WEBSITE ....

LOGIN ....

PASSWORD ....

NOTES ....

....

WEBSITE ....

LOGIN ....

PASSWORD ....

NOTES ....

....

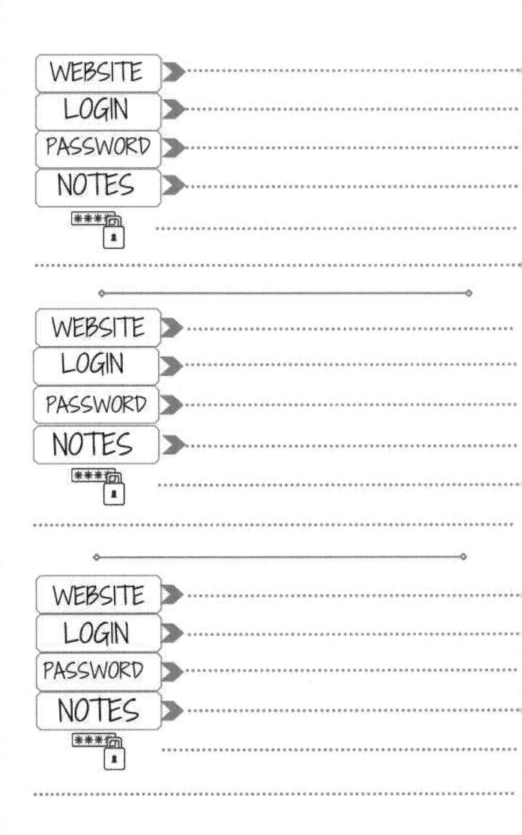

WEBSITE ▸ ....

LOGIN ▸ ....

PASSWORD ▸ ....

NOTES ▸ ....

....

....

WEBSITE ▸ ....

LOGIN ▸ ....

PASSWORD ▸ ....

NOTES ▸ ....

....

....

WEBSITE ▸ ....

LOGIN ▸ ....

PASSWORD ▸ ....

NOTES ▸ ....

....

....

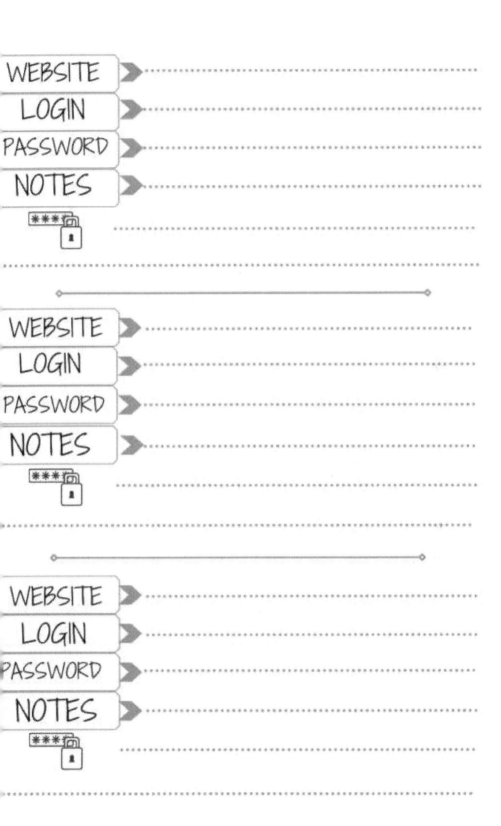

WEBSITE

LOGIN

PASSWORD

NOTES

WEBSITE

LOGIN

PASSWORD

NOTES

WEBSITE

LOGIN

PASSWORD

NOTES

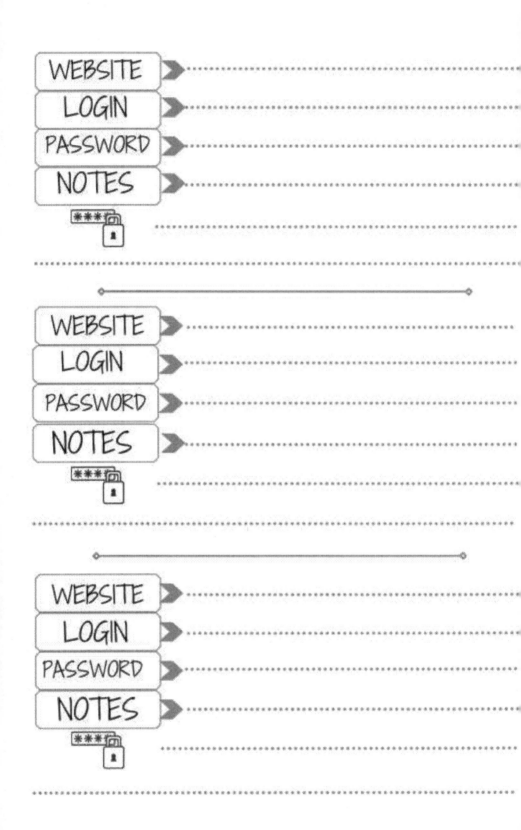

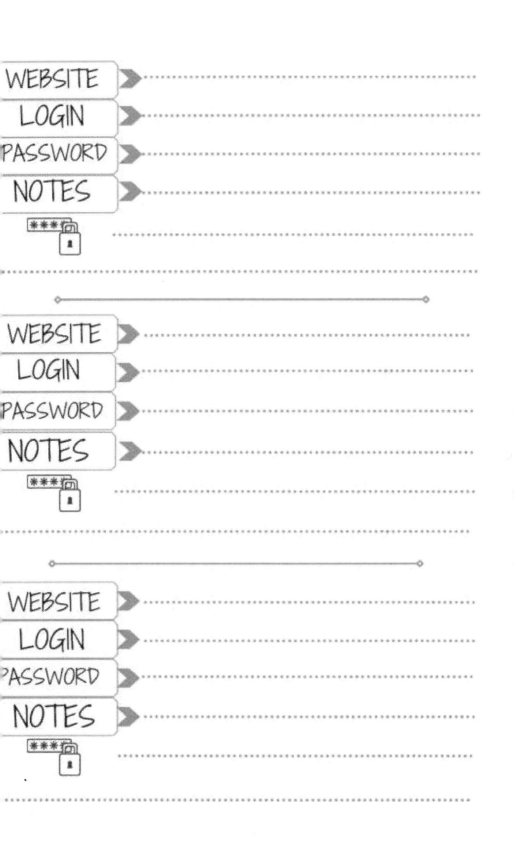

WEBSITE

LOGIN

PASSWORD

NOTES

WEBSITE

LOGIN

PASSWORD

NOTES

WEBSITE

LOGIN

PASSWORD

NOTES

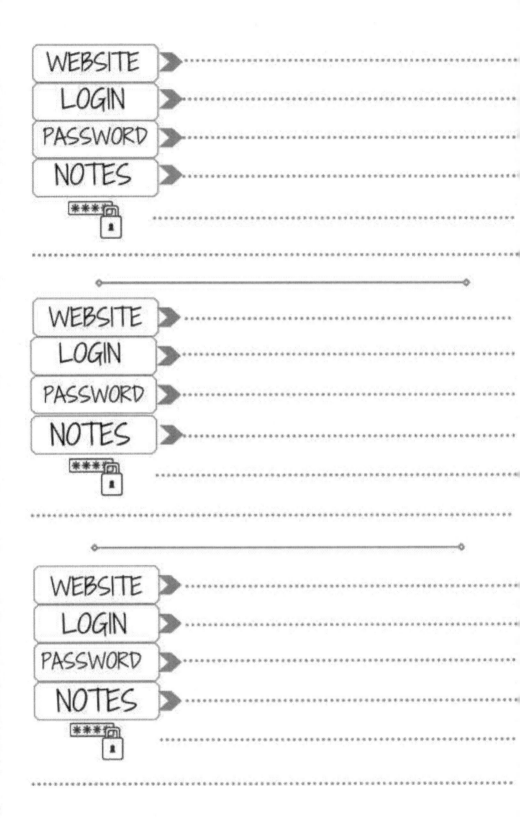

WEBSITE

LOGIN

PASSWORD

NOTES

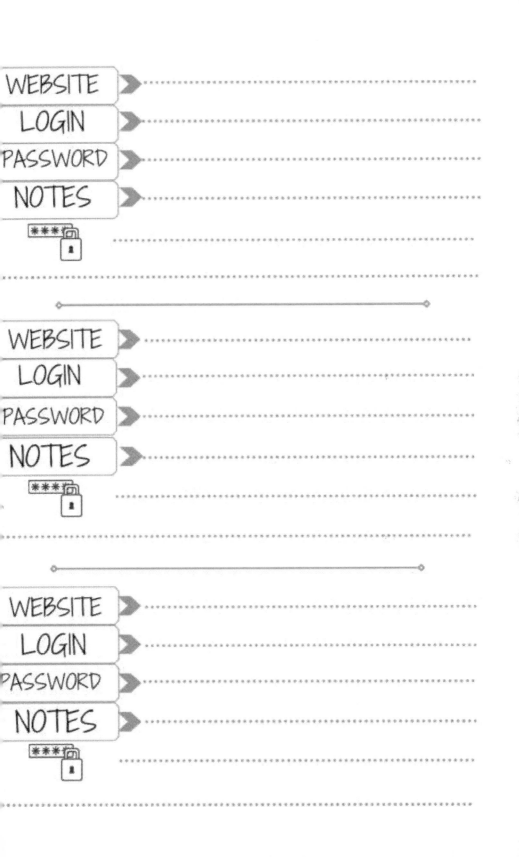

WEBSITE

LOGIN

PASSWORD

NOTES

WEBSITE

LOGIN

PASSWORD

NOTES

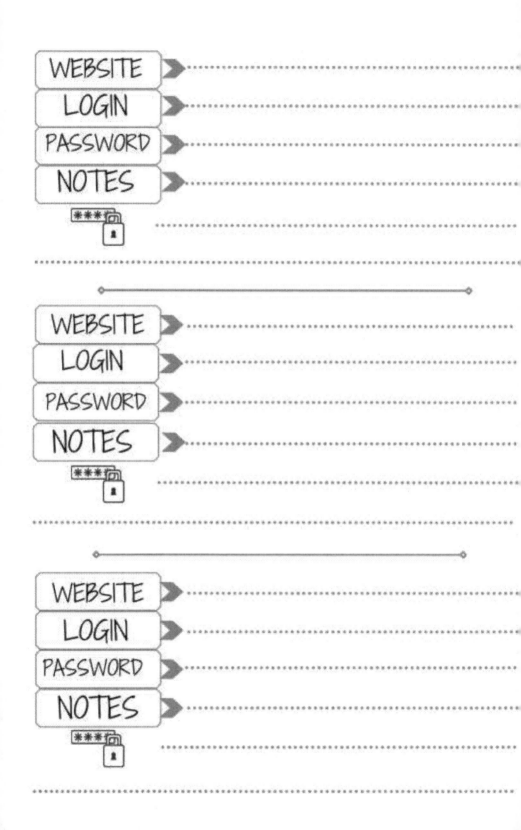

WEBSITE

LOGIN

PASSWORD

NOTES

WEBSITE

LOGIN

PASSWORD

NOTES

WEBSITE

LOGIN

PASSWORD

NOTES

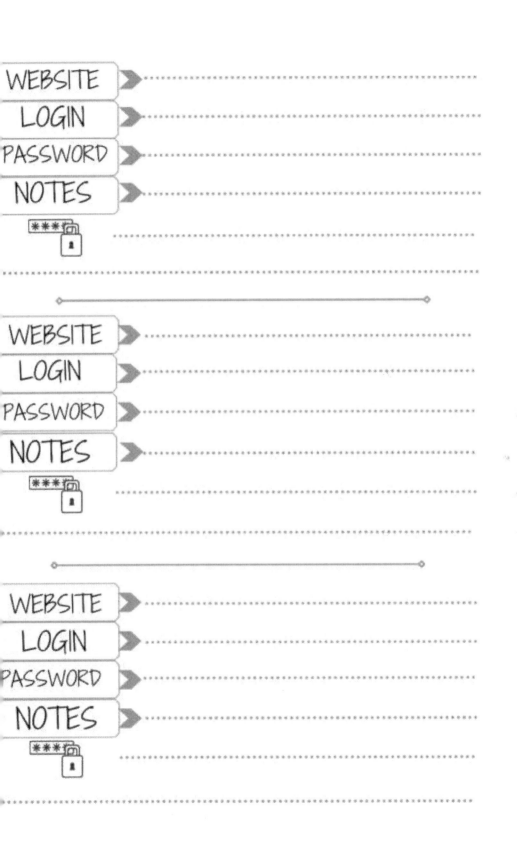

WEBSITE

LOGIN

PASSWORD

NOTES

WEBSITE

LOGIN

PASSWORD

NOTES

WEBSITE

LOGIN

PASSWORD

NOTES

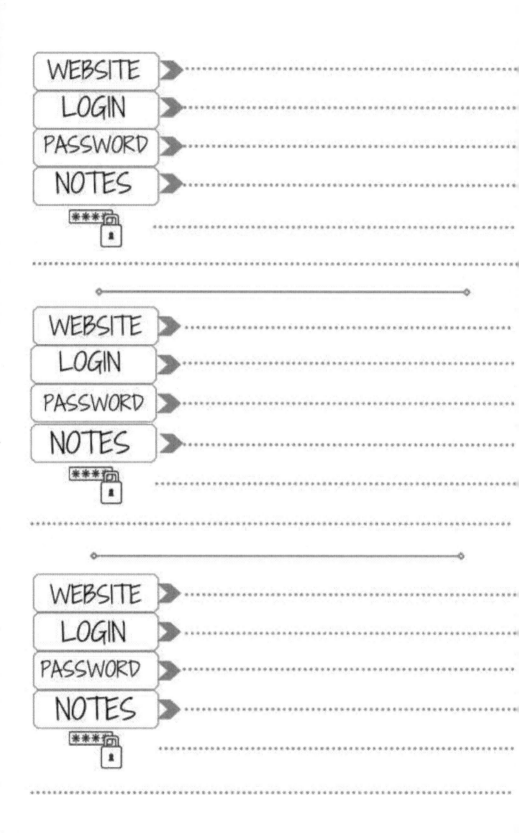

WEBSITE

LOGIN

PASSWORD

NOTES

WEBSITE

LOGIN

PASSWORD

NOTES

WEBSITE

LOGIN

PASSWORD

NOTES

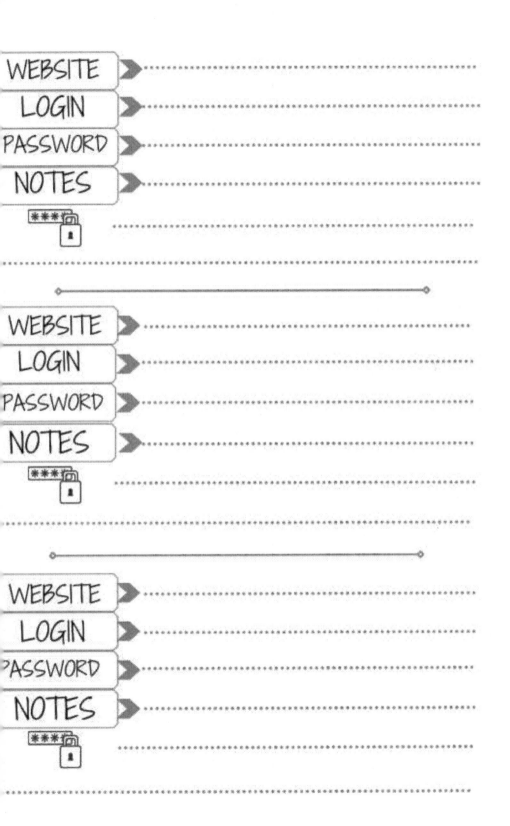

WEBSITE

LOGIN

PASSWORD

NOTES

WEBSITE

LOGIN

PASSWORD

NOTES

WEBSITE

LOGIN

PASSWORD

NOTES

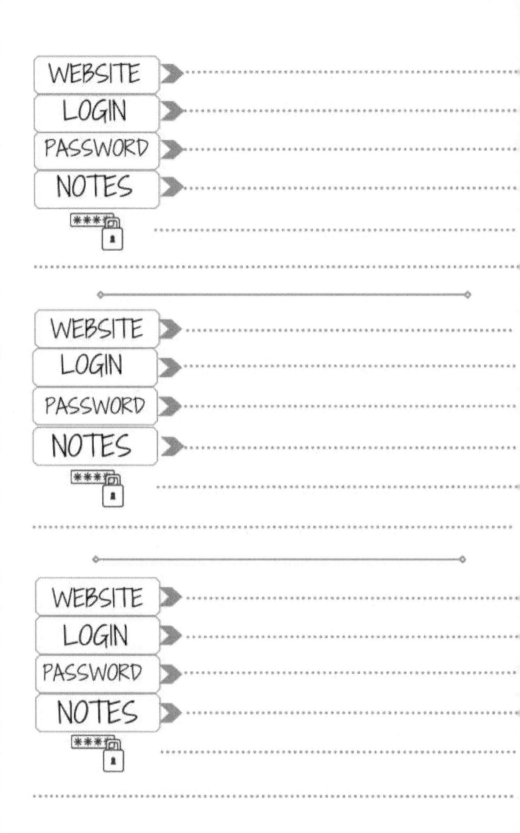

WEBSITE

LOGIN

PASSWORD

NOTES

WEBSITE

LOGIN

PASSWORD

NOTES

WEBSITE

LOGIN

PASSWORD

NOTES

WEBSITE

LOGIN

PASSWORD

NOTES

***

WEBSITE

LOGIN

PASSWORD

NOTES

***

WEBSITE

LOGIN

PASSWORD

NOTES

***

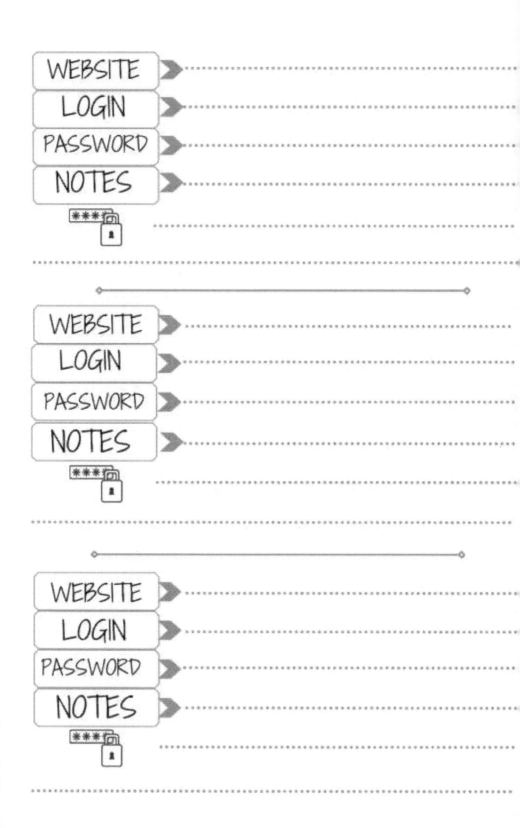

WEBSITE

LOGIN

PASSWORD

NOTES

WEBSITE

LOGIN

PASSWORD

NOTES

WEBSITE

LOGIN

PASSWORD

NOTES

WEBSITE ....

LOGIN ....

PASSWORD ....

NOTES ....

***..

....

WEBSITE ....

LOGIN ....

PASSWORD ....

NOTES ....

***..

....

WEBSITE ....

LOGIN ....

PASSWORD ....

NOTES ....

***..

....

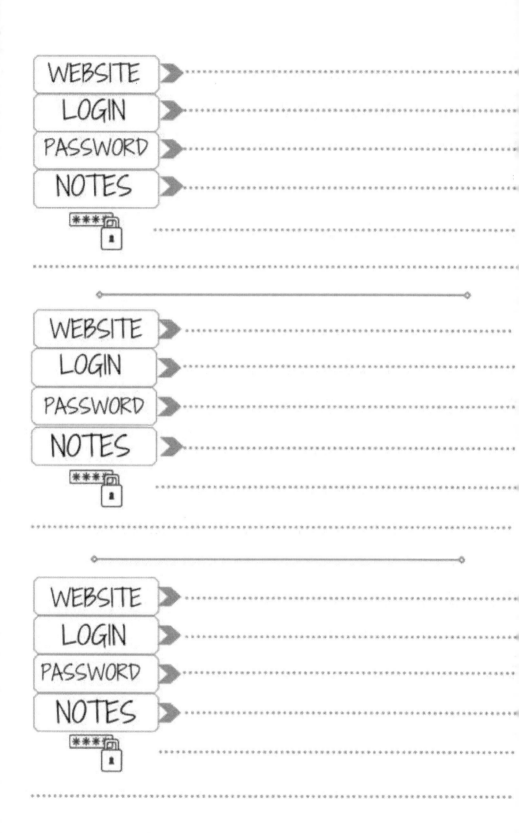

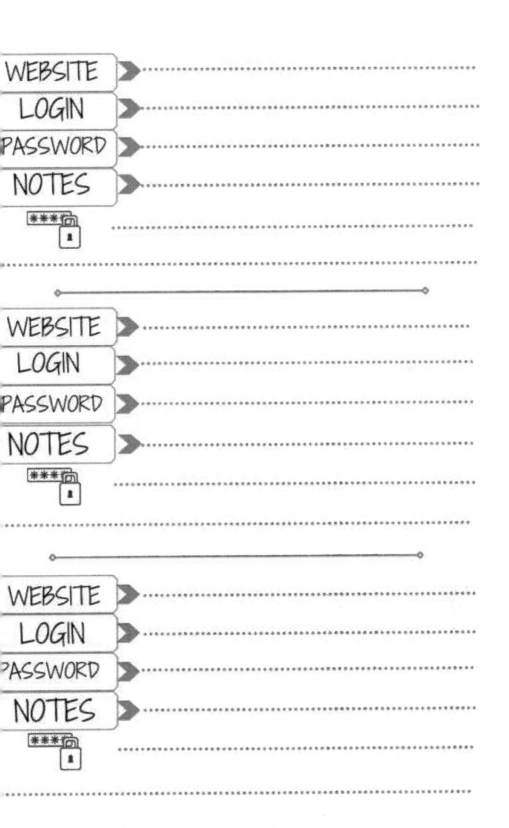

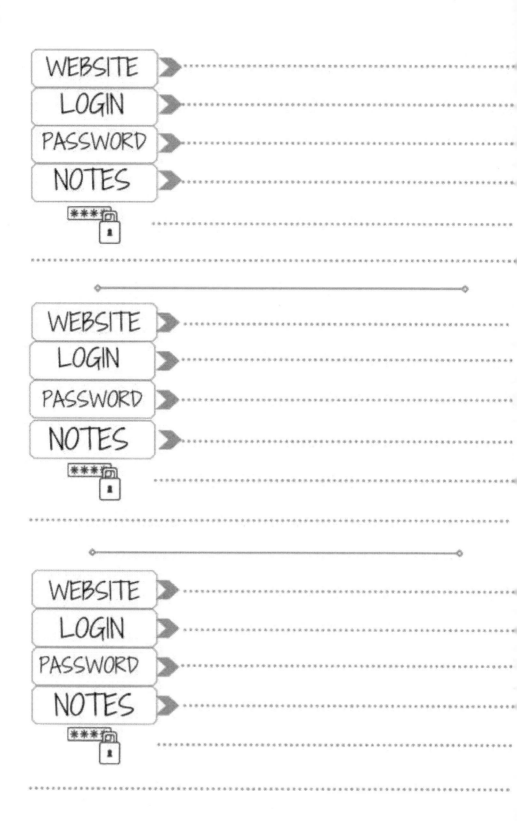

WEBSITE

LOGIN

PASSWORD

NOTES

WEBSITE

LOGIN

PASSWORD

NOTES

WEBSITE

LOGIN

PASSWORD

NOTES

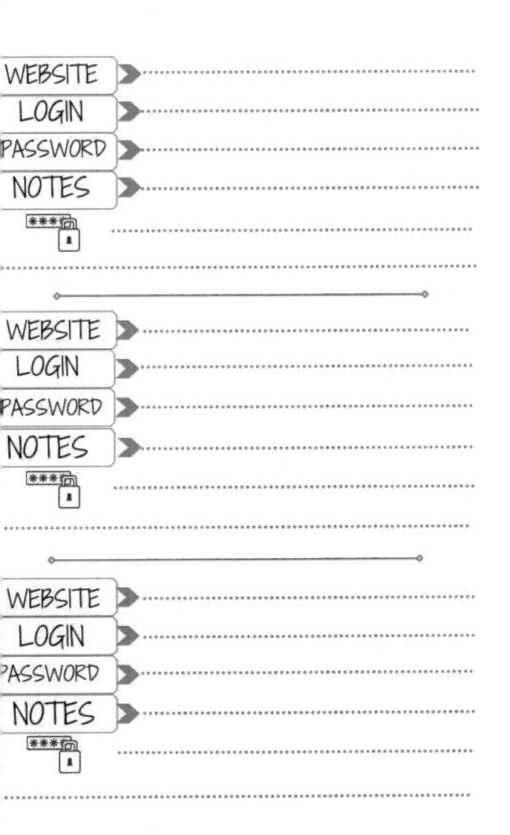

WEBSITE

LOGIN

PASSWORD

NOTES

WEBSITE

LOGIN

PASSWORD

NOTES

WEBSITE

LOGIN

PASSWORD

NOTES

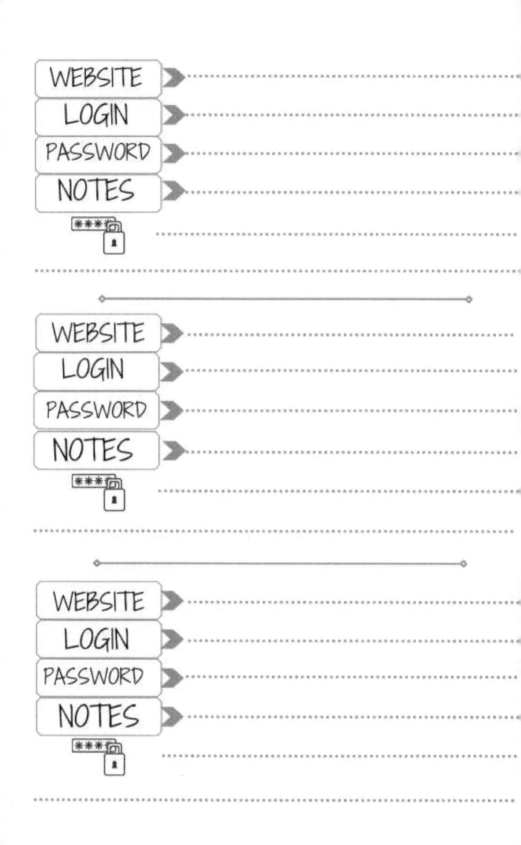

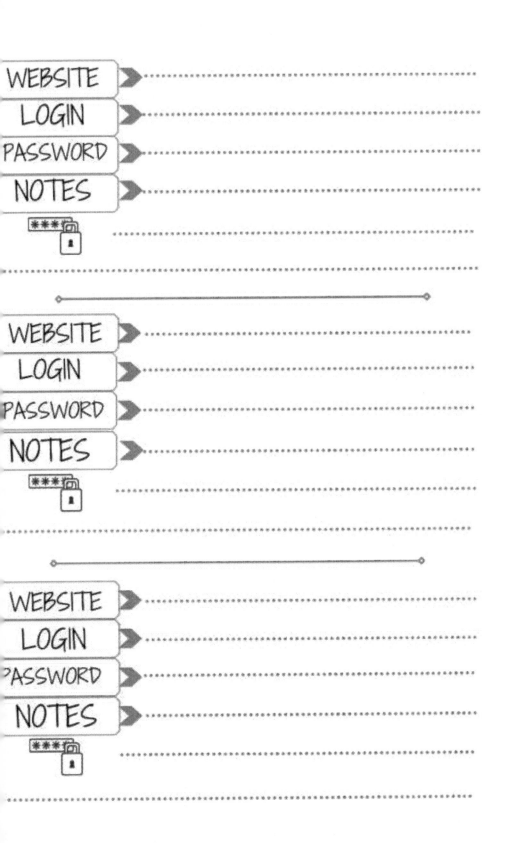

WEBSITE

LOGIN

PASSWORD

NOTES

WEBSITE

LOGIN

PASSWORD

NOTES

WEBSITE

LOGIN

PASSWORD

NOTES

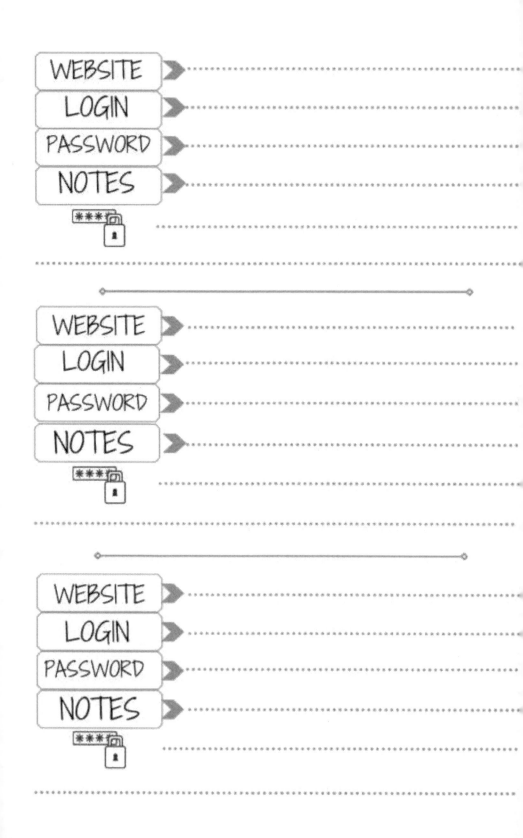

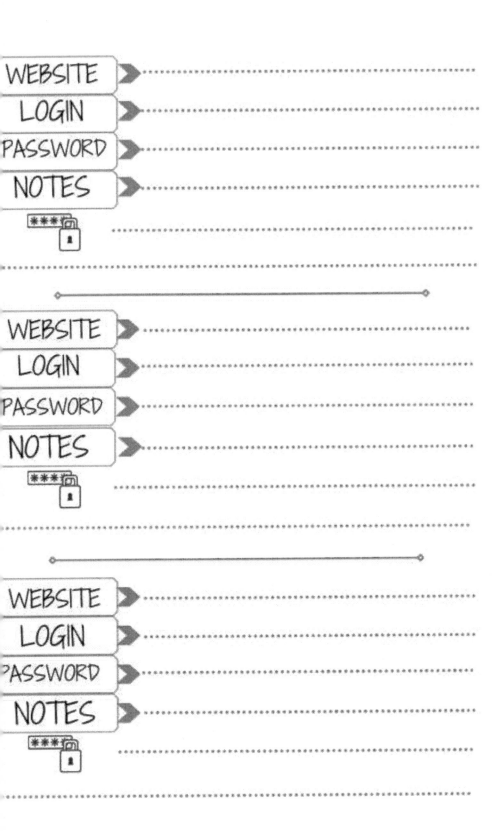

WEBSITE

LOGIN

PASSWORD

NOTES

WEBSITE

LOGIN

PASSWORD

NOTES

WEBSITE

LOGIN

PASSWORD

NOTES

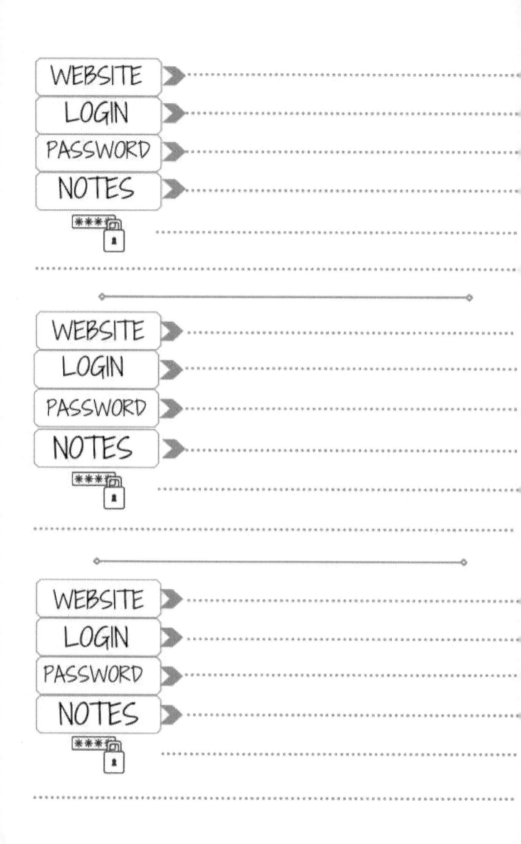

WEBSITE

LOGIN

PASSWORD

NOTES

WEBSITE

LOGIN

PASSWORD

NOTES

WEBSITE

LOGIN

PASSWORD

NOTES

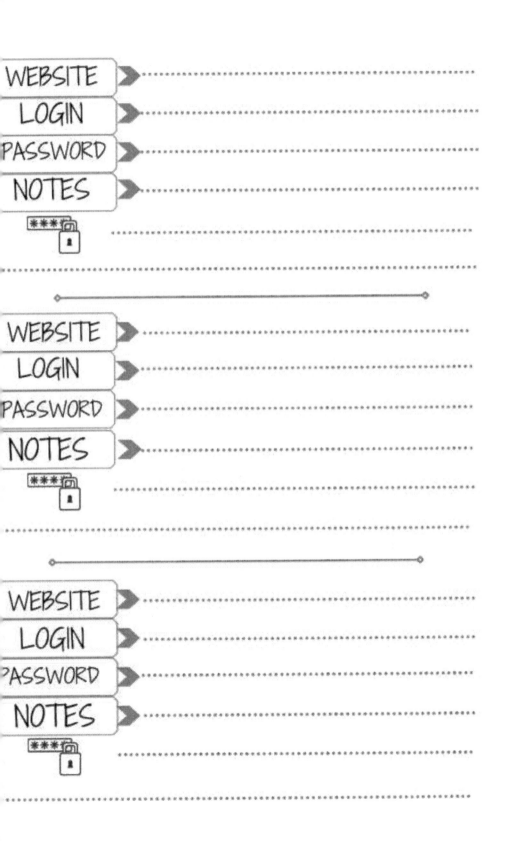

WEBSITE

LOGIN

PASSWORD

NOTES

WEBSITE

LOGIN

PASSWORD

NOTES

WEBSITE

LOGIN

PASSWORD

NOTES

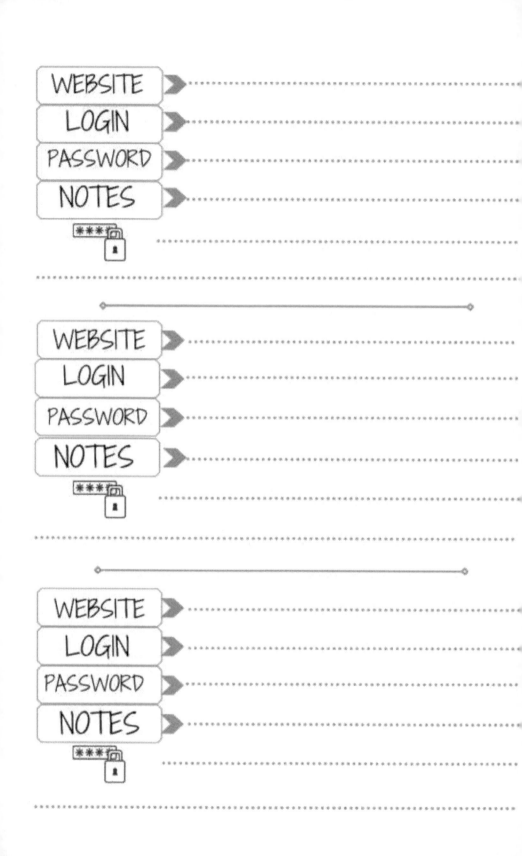

WEBSITE ⟩ ··

LOGIN ⟩ ··

PASSWORD ⟩ ··

NOTES ⟩ ··

··

WEBSITE ⟩ ··

LOGIN ⟩ ··

PASSWORD ⟩ ··

NOTES ⟩ ··

··

WEBSITE ⟩ ··

LOGIN ⟩ ··

PASSWORD ⟩ ··

NOTES ⟩ ··

··

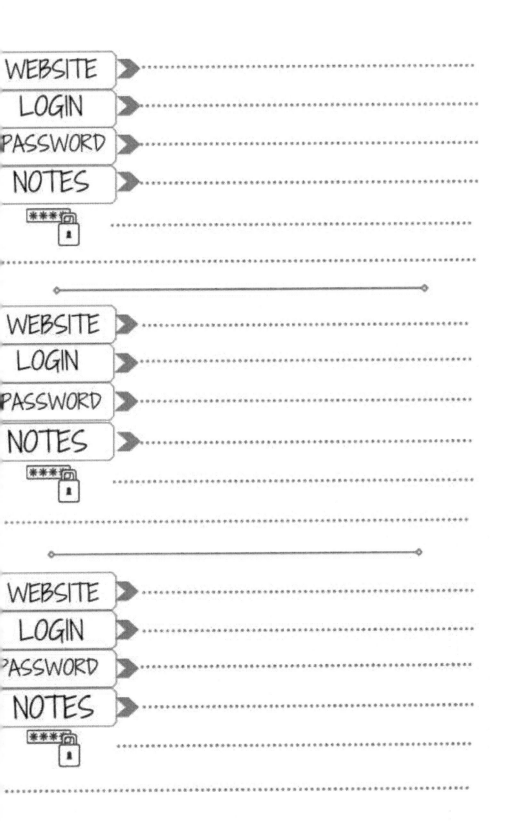

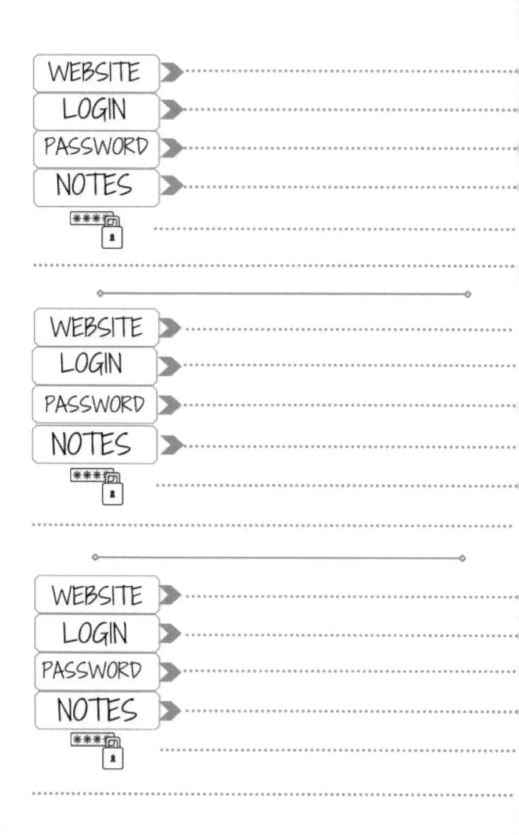

WEBSITE

LOGIN

PASSWORD

NOTES

WEBSITE

LOGIN

PASSWORD

NOTES

WEBSITE

LOGIN

PASSWORD

NOTES

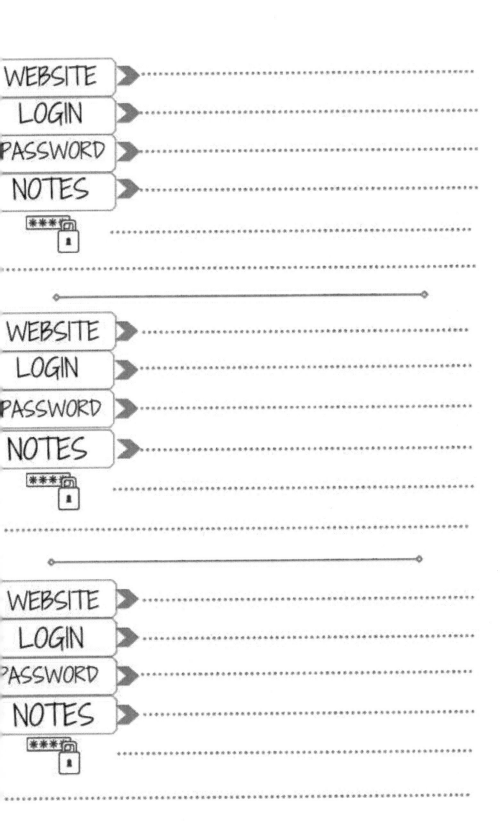

WEBSITE ....

LOGIN ....

PASSWORD ....

NOTES ....

....

WEBSITE ....

LOGIN ....

PASSWORD ....

NOTES ....

....

WEBSITE ....

LOGIN ....

PASSWORD ....

NOTES ....

....

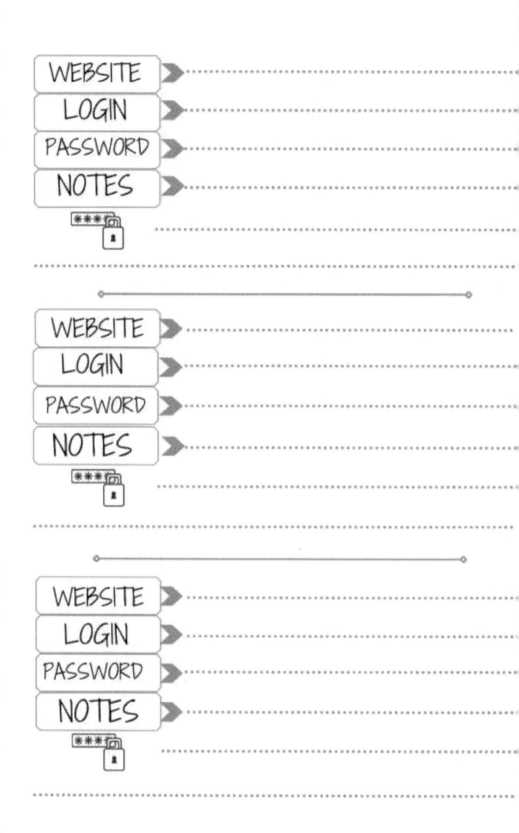

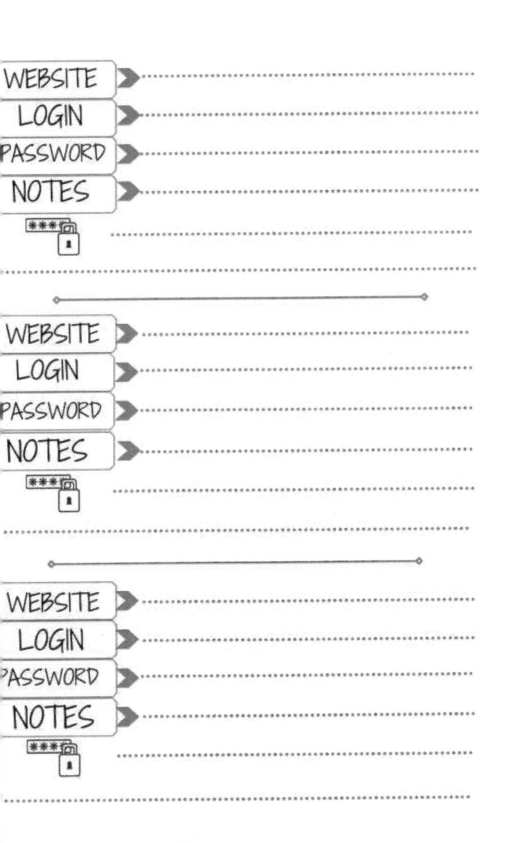

WEBSITE

LOGIN

PASSWORD

NOTES

WEBSITE

LOGIN

PASSWORD

NOTES

WEBSITE

LOGIN

PASSWORD

NOTES

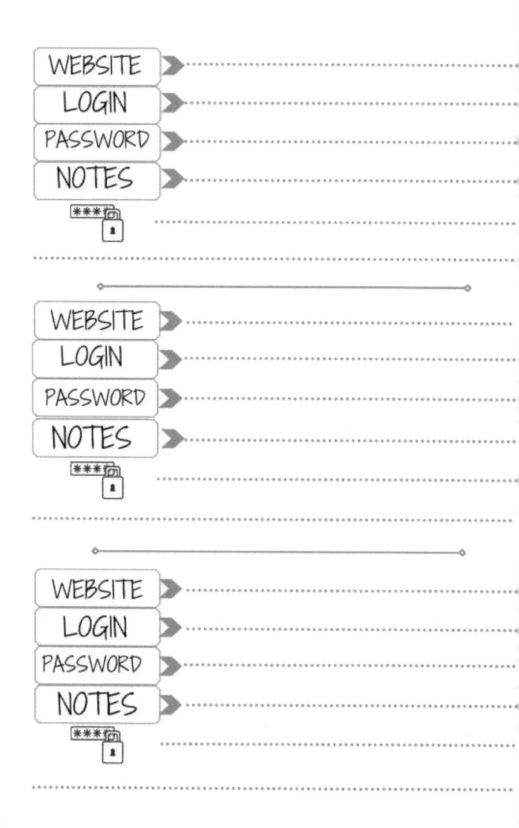

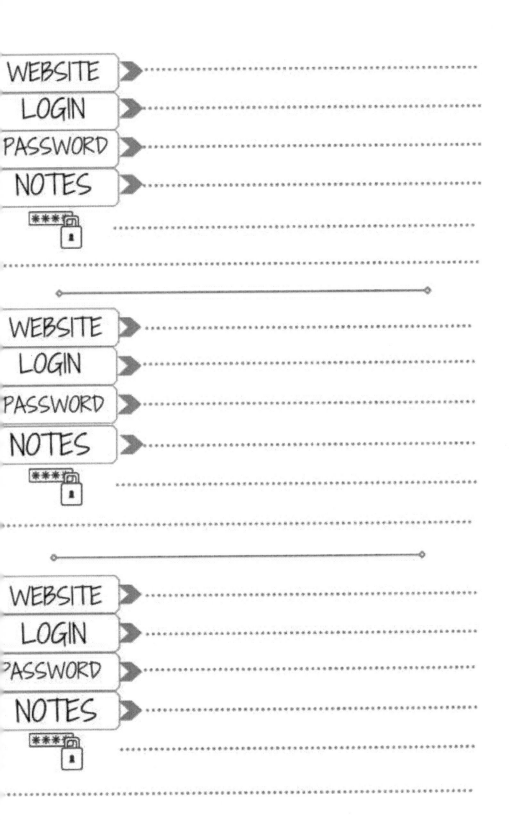

WEBSITE ⟩ ....

LOGIN ⟩ ....

PASSWORD ⟩ ....

NOTES ⟩ ....

....

....

WEBSITE ⟩ ....

LOGIN ⟩ ....

PASSWORD ⟩ ....

NOTES ⟩ ....

....

....

WEBSITE ⟩ ....

LOGIN ⟩ ....

PASSWORD ⟩ ....

NOTES ⟩ ....

....

....

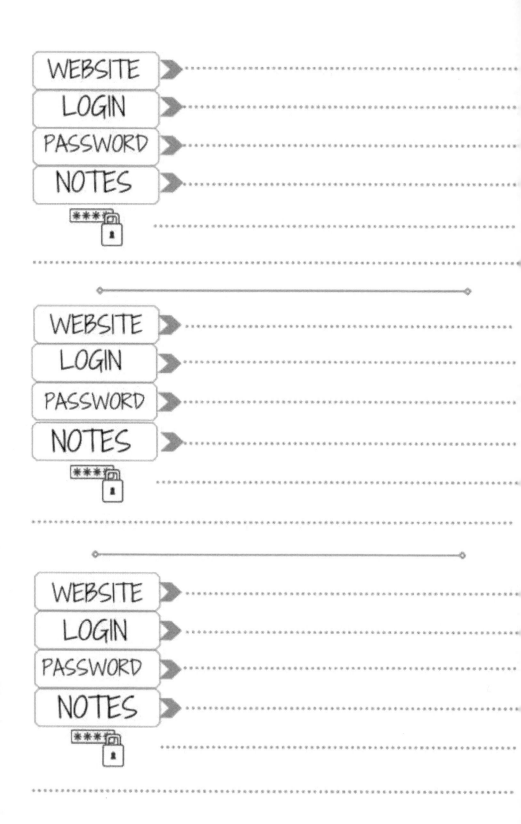

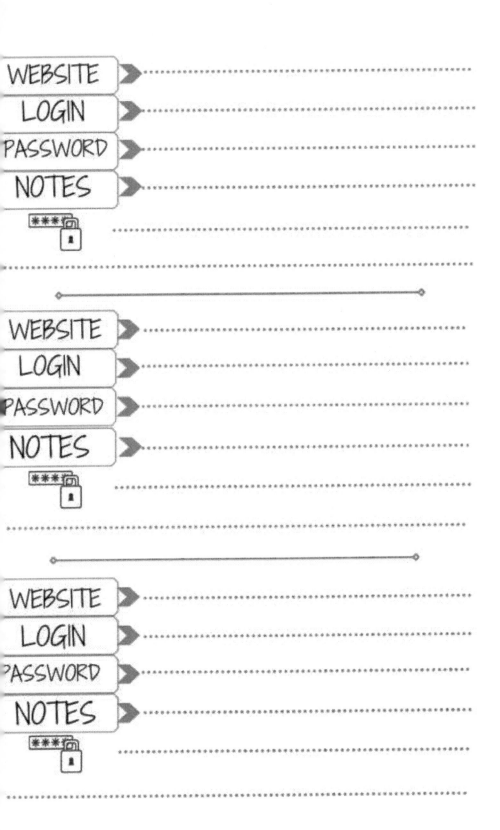

WEBSITE ....

LOGIN ....

PASSWORD ....

NOTES ....

WEBSITE ....

LOGIN ....

PASSWORD ....

NOTES ....

WEBSITE ....

LOGIN ....

PASSWORD ....

NOTES ....

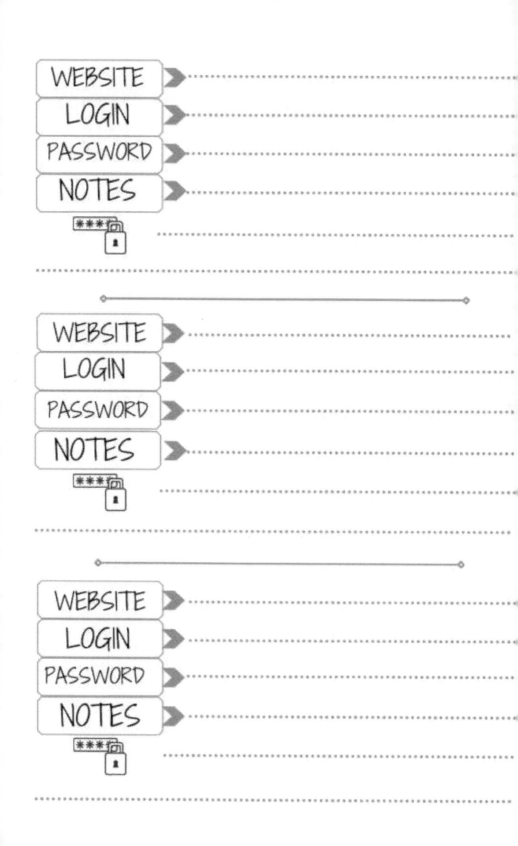

WEBSITE

LOGIN

PASSWORD

NOTES

WEBSITE

LOGIN

PASSWORD

NOTES

WEBSITE

LOGIN

PASSWORD

NOTES

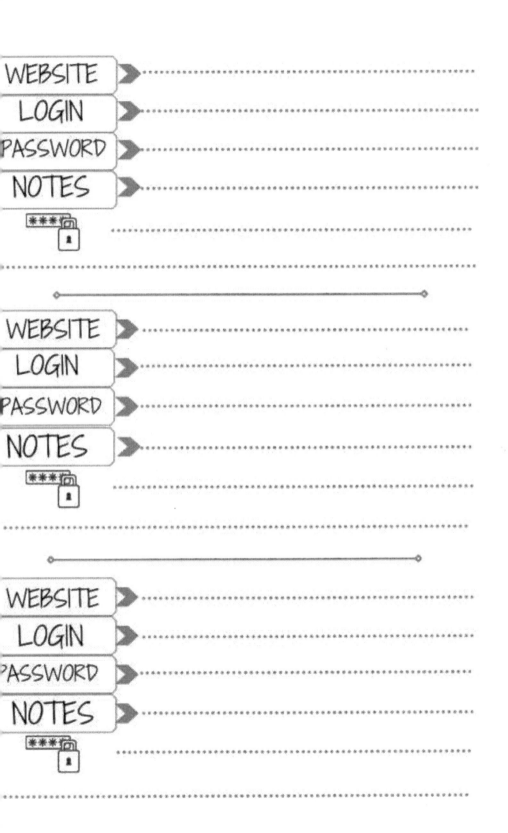

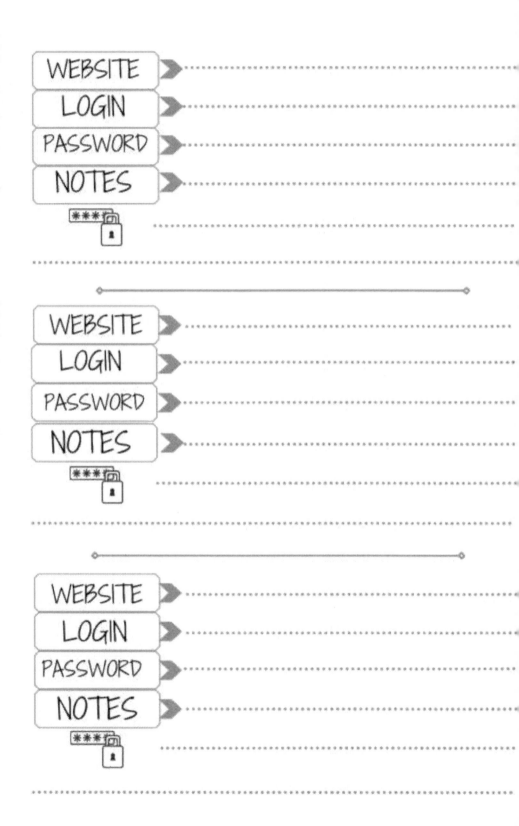

WEBSITE

LOGIN

PASSWORD

NOTES

WEBSITE

LOGIN

PASSWORD

NOTES

WEBSITE

LOGIN

PASSWORD

NOTES

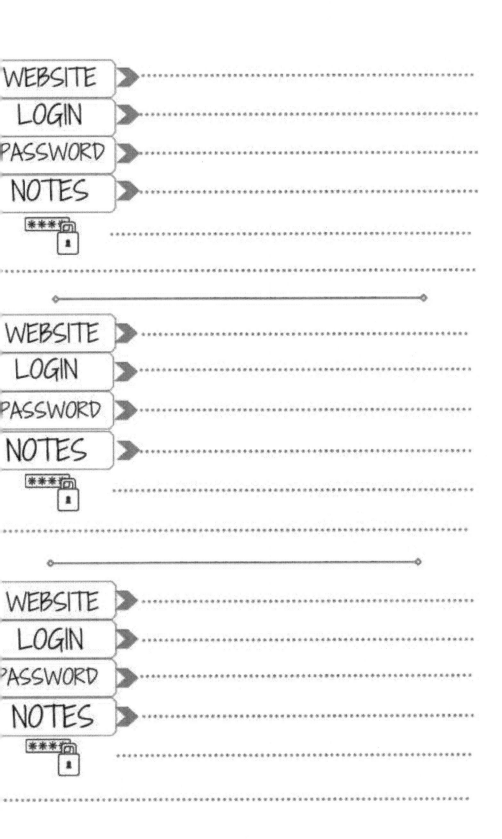

WEBSITE ....

LOGIN ....

PASSWORD ....

NOTES ....

****🔒 ....
🔒

....

WEBSITE ....

LOGIN ....

PASSWORD ....

NOTES ....

****🔒 ....
🔒

....

WEBSITE ....

LOGIN ....

PASSWORD ....

NOTES ....

****🔒 ....
🔒

....

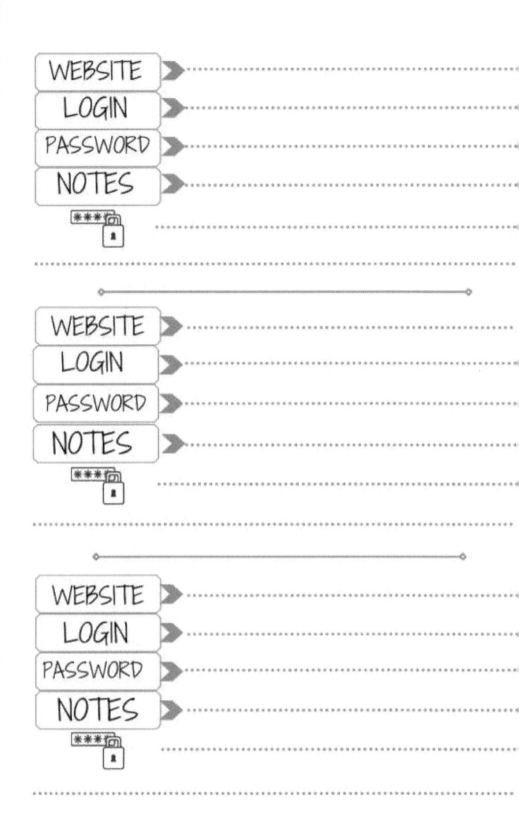

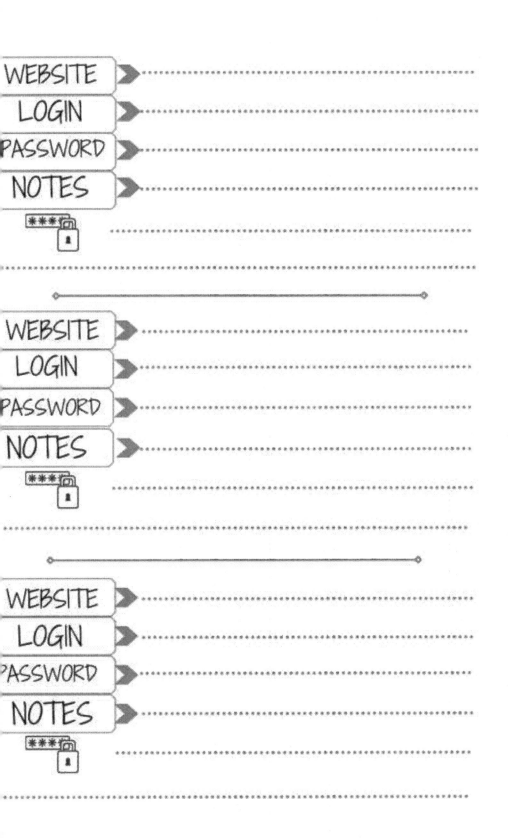

WEBSITE ....

LOGIN ....

PASSWORD ....

NOTES ....

....

....

WEBSITE ....

LOGIN ....

PASSWORD ....

NOTES ....

....

....

WEBSITE ....

LOGIN ....

PASSWORD ....

NOTES ....

....

....

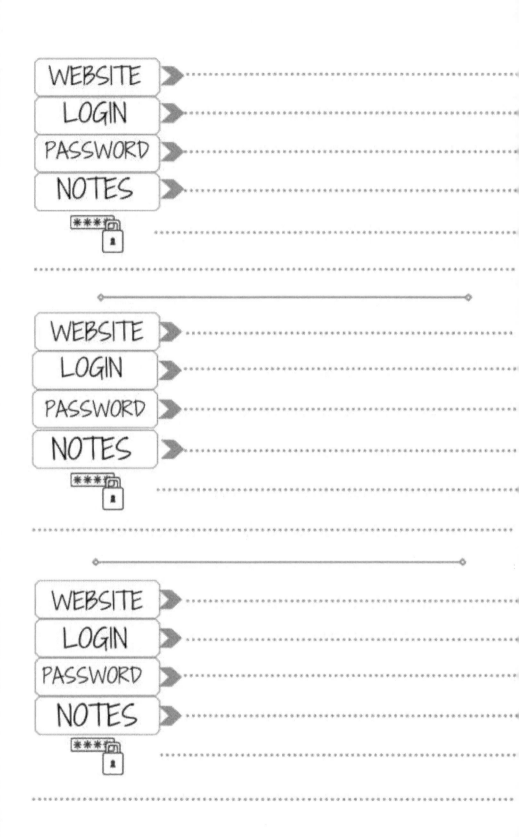

WEBSITE

LOGIN

PASSWORD

NOTES

WEBSITE

LOGIN

PASSWORD

NOTES

WEBSITE

LOGIN

PASSWORD

NOTES

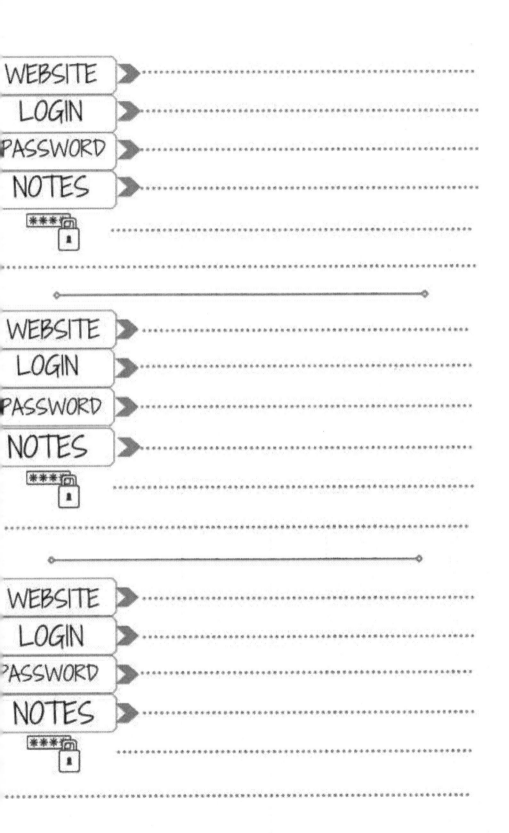

WEBSITE ....

LOGIN ....

PASSWORD ....

NOTES ....

....

....

WEBSITE ....

LOGIN ....

PASSWORD ....

NOTES ....

....

....

WEBSITE ....

LOGIN ....

PASSWORD ....

NOTES ....

....

....

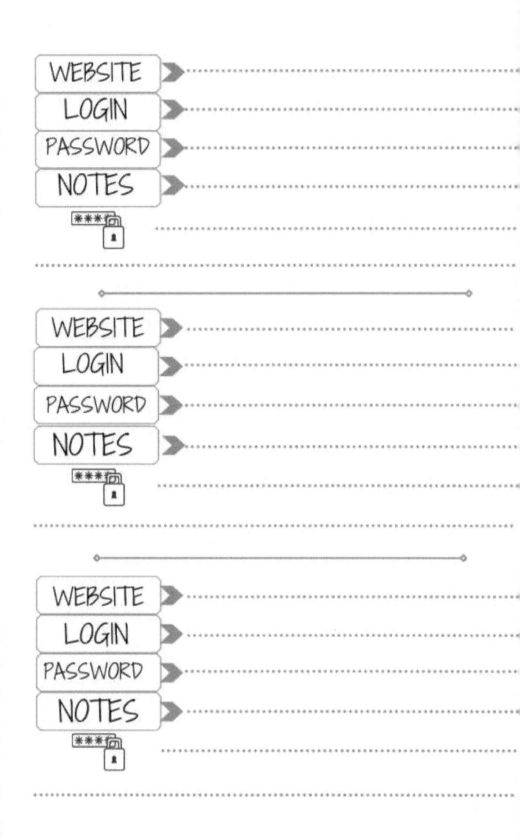

WEBSITE

LOGIN

PASSWORD

NOTES

WEBSITE

LOGIN

PASSWORD

NOTES

WEBSITE

LOGIN

PASSWORD

NOTES

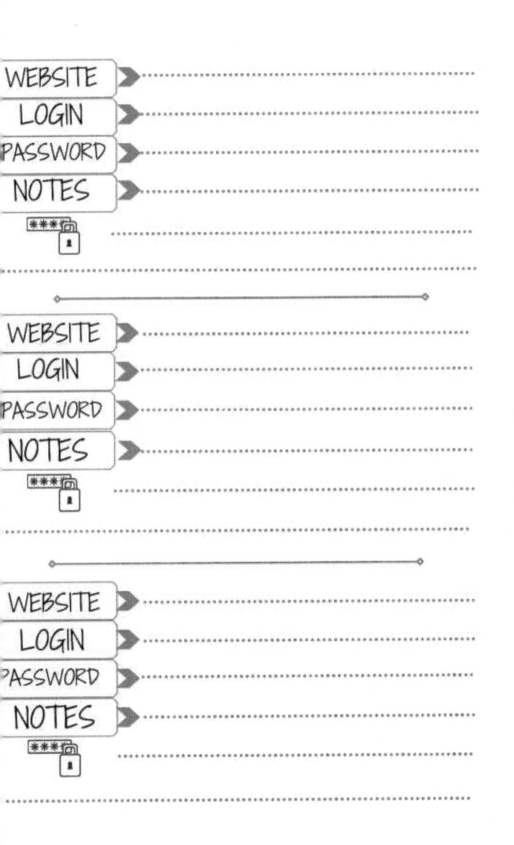

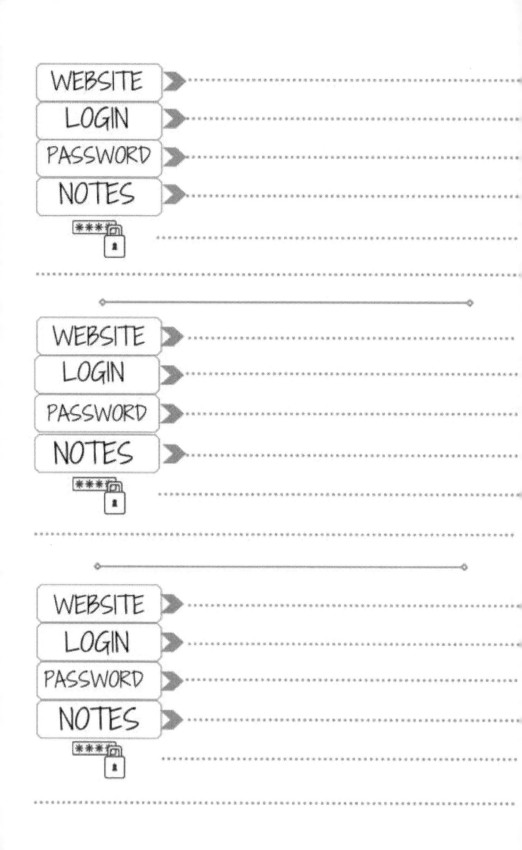

WEBSITE

LOGIN

PASSWORD

NOTES

WEBSITE

LOGIN

PASSWORD

NOTES

WEBSITE

LOGIN

PASSWORD

NOTES

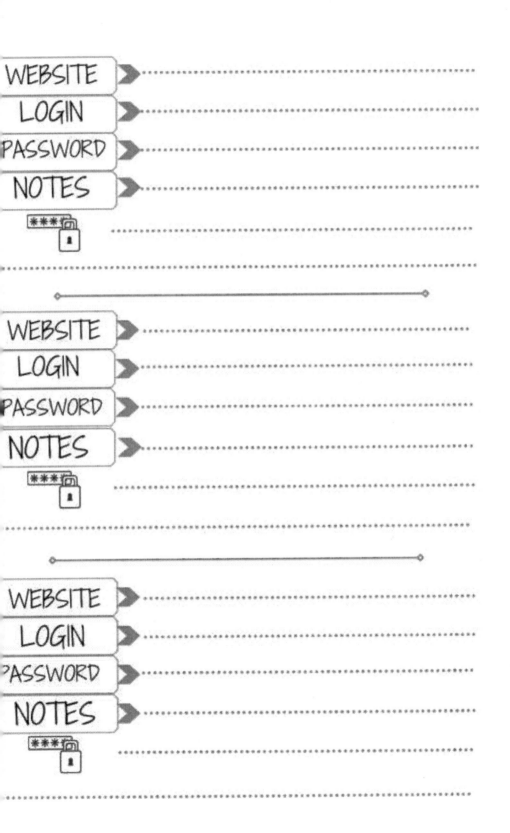

WEBSITE
LOGIN
PASSWORD
NOTES

WEBSITE
LOGIN
PASSWORD
NOTES

WEBSITE
LOGIN
PASSWORD
NOTES

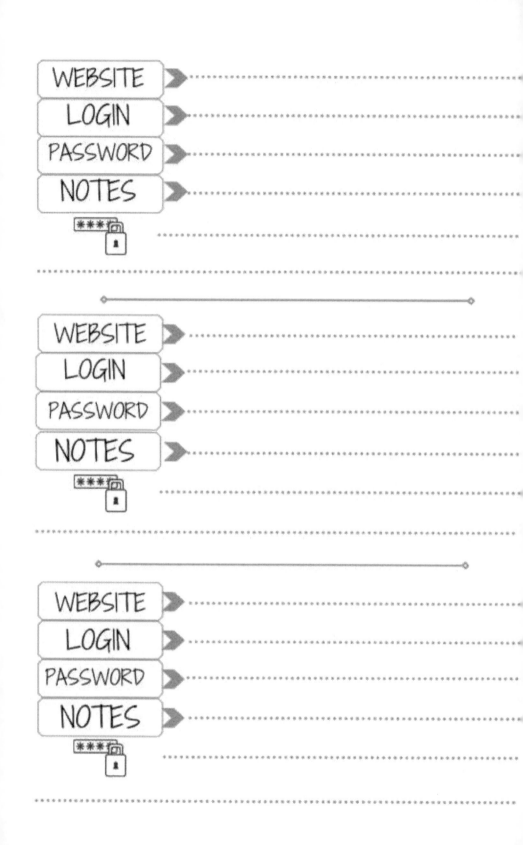

WEBSITE ....

LOGIN ....

PASSWORD ....

NOTES ....

....

WEBSITE ....

LOGIN ....

PASSWORD ....

NOTES ....

....

WEBSITE ....

LOGIN ....

PASSWORD ....

NOTES ....

....

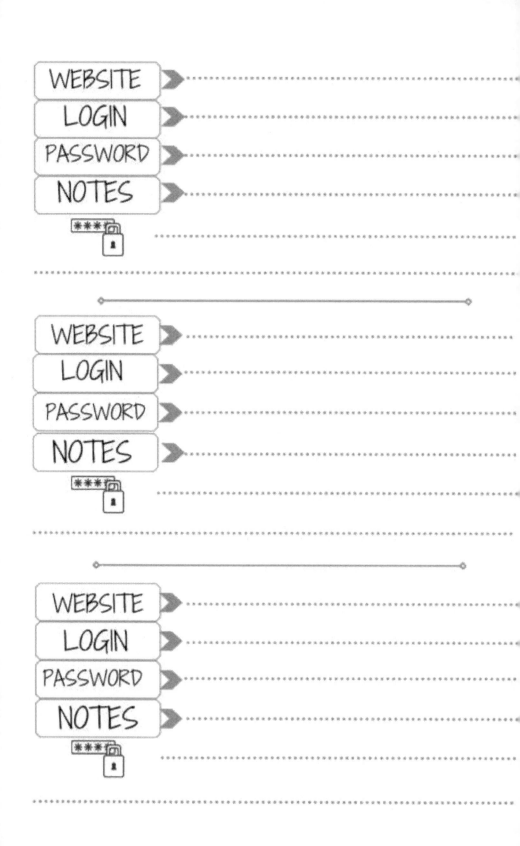

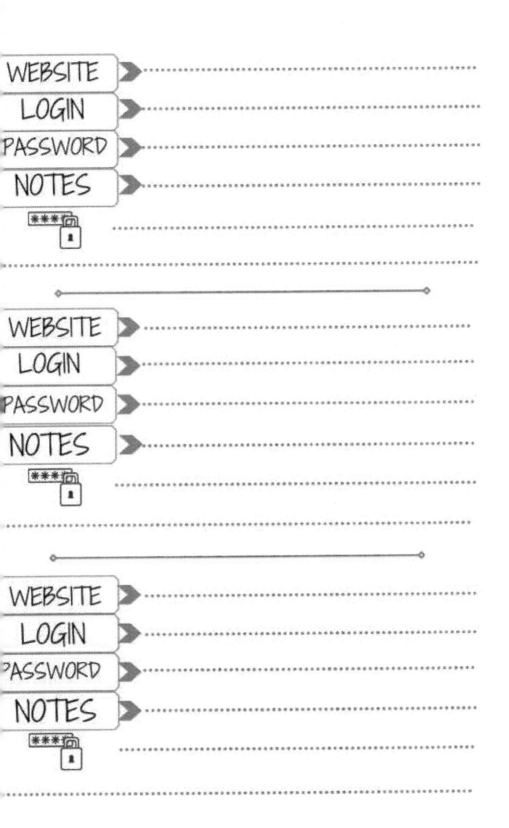

WEBSITE

LOGIN

PASSWORD

NOTES

WEBSITE

LOGIN

PASSWORD

NOTES

WEBSITE

LOGIN

PASSWORD

NOTES

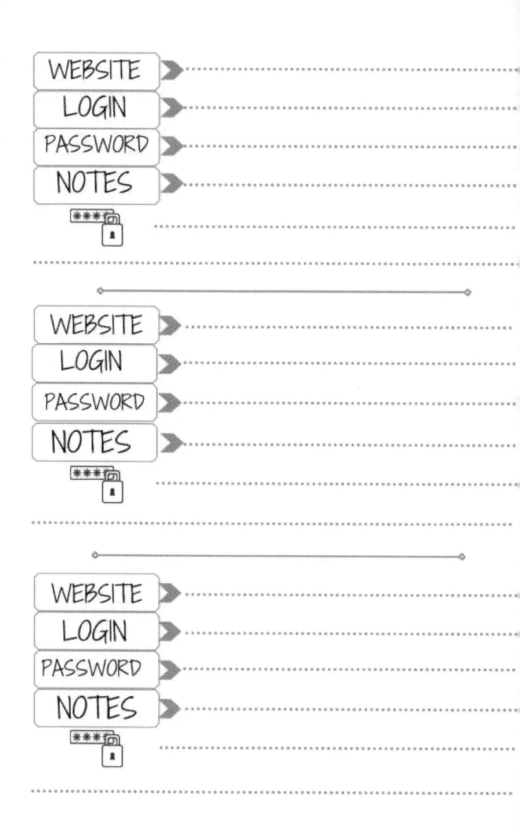

WEBSITE

LOGIN

PASSWORD

NOTES

WEBSITE

LOGIN

PASSWORD

NOTES

WEBSITE

LOGIN

PASSWORD

NOTES

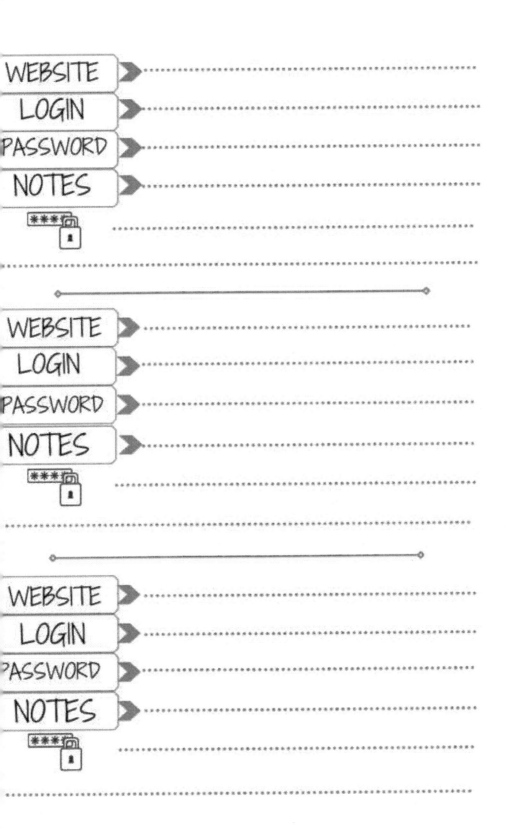

WEBSITE

LOGIN

PASSWORD

NOTES

WEBSITE

LOGIN

PASSWORD

NOTES

WEBSITE

LOGIN

PASSWORD

NOTES

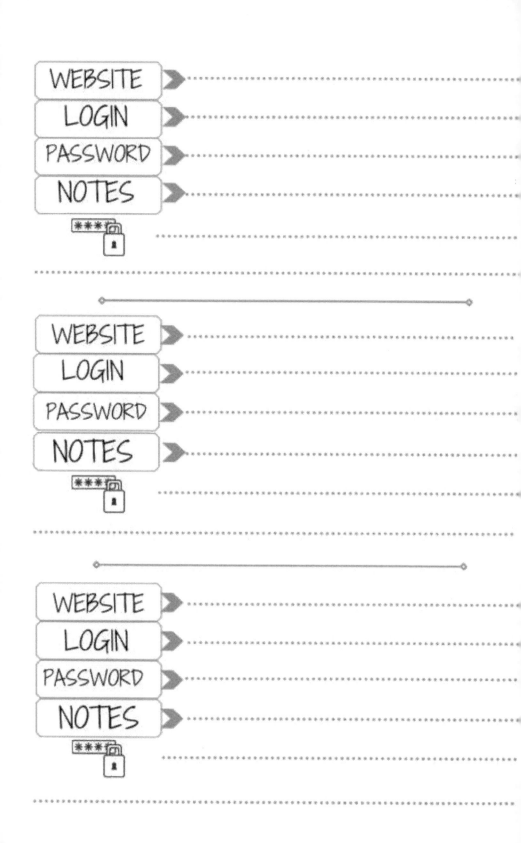

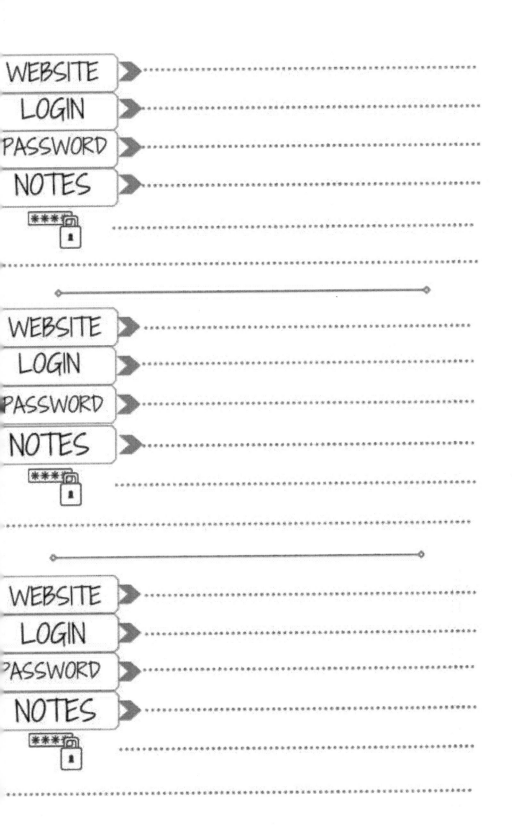

WEBSITE ....

LOGIN ....

PASSWORD ....

NOTES ....

***🔒
🔒 ....

....

WEBSITE ....

LOGIN ....

PASSWORD ....

NOTES ....

***🔒
🔒 ....

....

WEBSITE ....

LOGIN ....

PASSWORD ....

NOTES ....

***🔒
🔒 ....

....

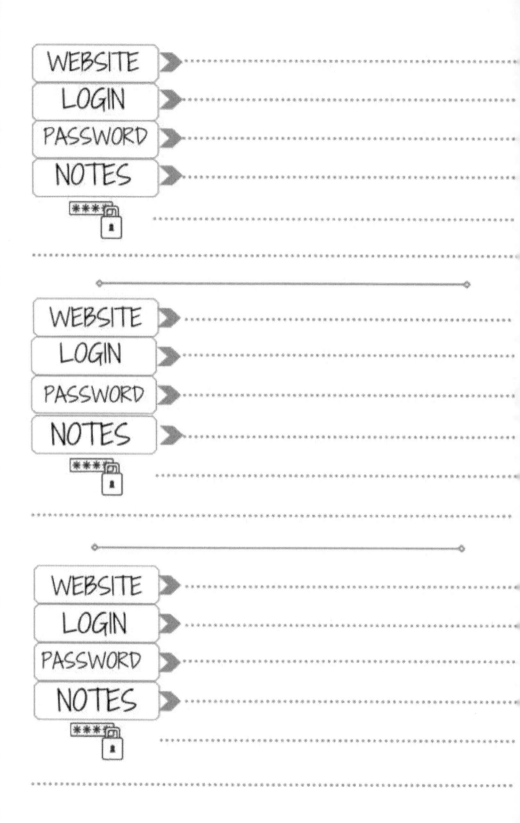

WEBSITE ▸ ....

LOGIN ▸ ....

PASSWORD ▸ ....

NOTES ▸ ....

....

WEBSITE ▸ ....

LOGIN ▸ ....

PASSWORD ▸ ....

NOTES ▸ ....

....

WEBSITE ▸ ....

LOGIN ▸ ....

PASSWORD ▸ ....

NOTES ▸ ....

....

WEBSITE ....

LOGIN ....

PASSWORD ....

NOTES ....

****
....

....

WEBSITE ....

LOGIN ....

PASSWORD ....

NOTES ....

****
....

....

WEBSITE ....

LOGIN ....

PASSWORD ....

NOTES ....

****
....

....

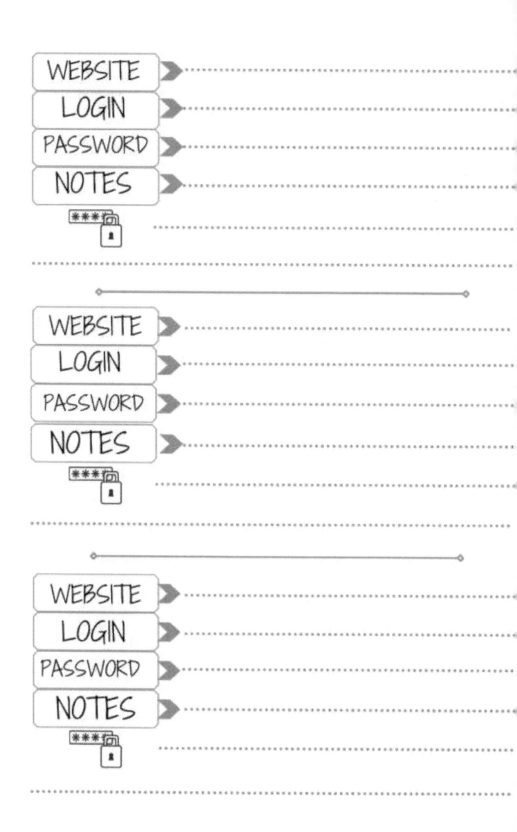

WEBSITE

LOGIN

PASSWORD

NOTES

WEBSITE

LOGIN

PASSWORD

NOTES

WEBSITE

LOGIN

PASSWORD

NOTES

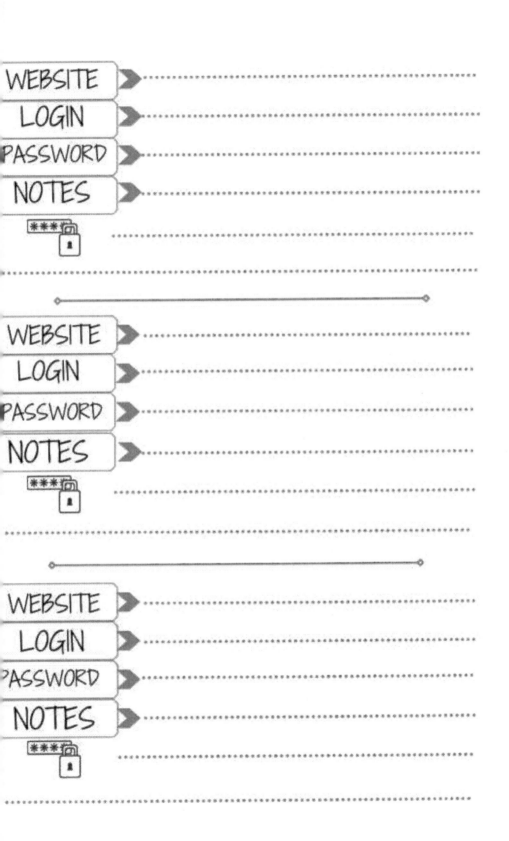

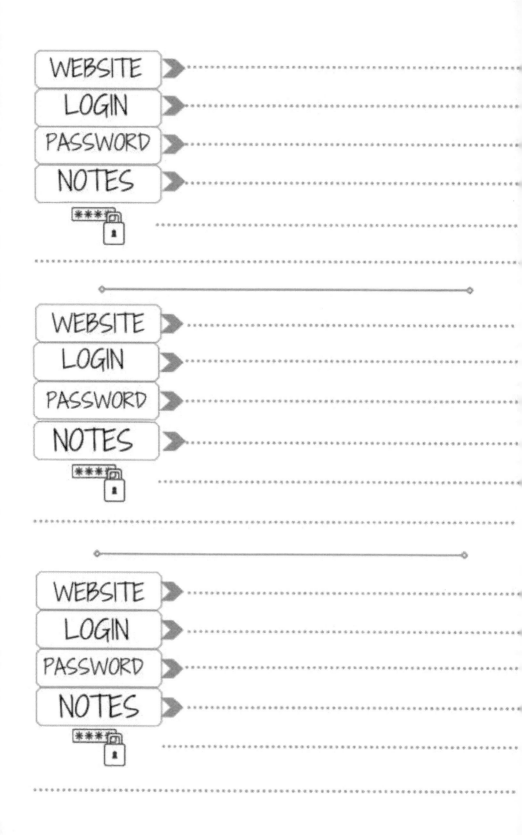

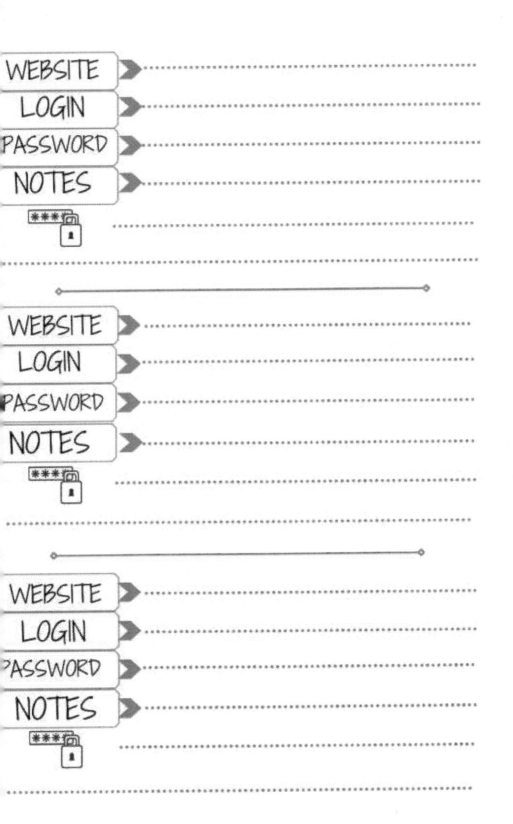

WEBSITE ....

LOGIN ....

PASSWORD ....

NOTES ....

****🔒 ....

WEBSITE ....

LOGIN ....

PASSWORD ....

NOTES ....

****🔒 ....

WEBSITE ....

LOGIN ....

PASSWORD ....

NOTES ....

****🔒 ....

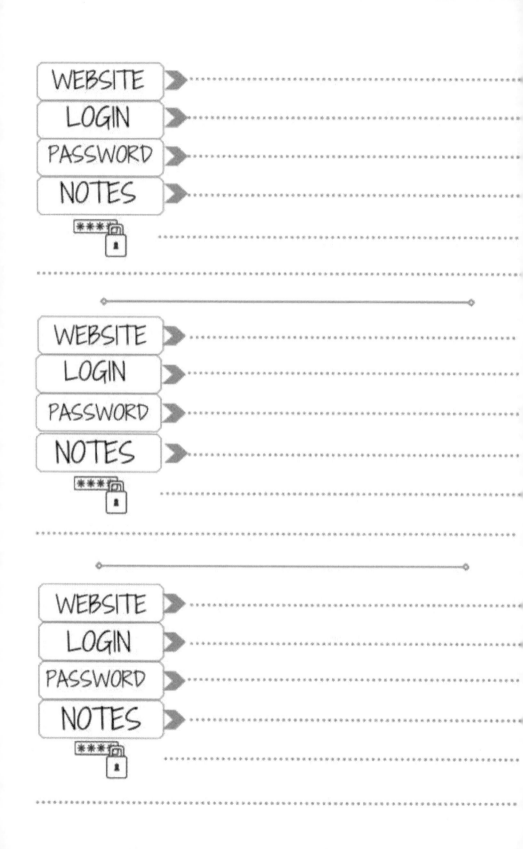

WEBSITE ▶ ....

LOGIN ▶ ....

PASSWORD ▶ ....

NOTES ▶ ....

....

WEBSITE ▶ ....

LOGIN ▶ ....

PASSWORD ▶ ....

NOTES ▶ ....

....

WEBSITE ▶ ....

LOGIN ▶ ....

PASSWORD ▶ ....

NOTES ▶ ....

....

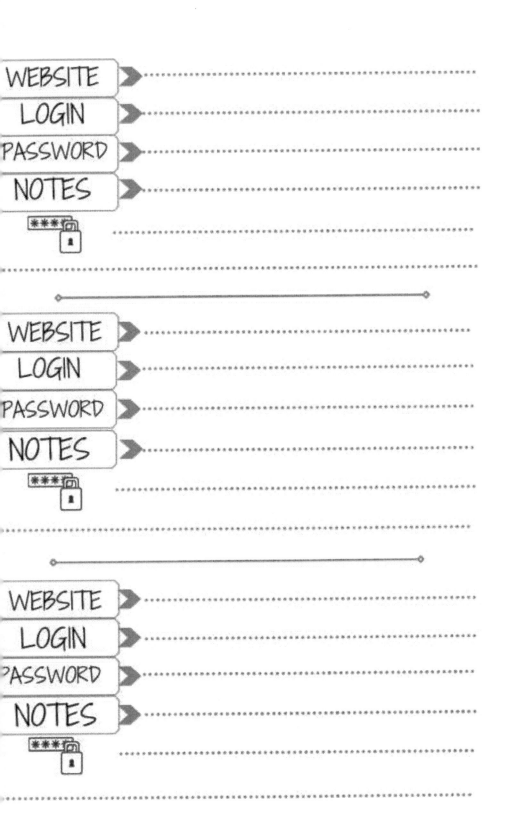

WEBSITE

LOGIN

PASSWORD

NOTES

WEBSITE

LOGIN

PASSWORD

NOTES

WEBSITE

LOGIN

PASSWORD

NOTES

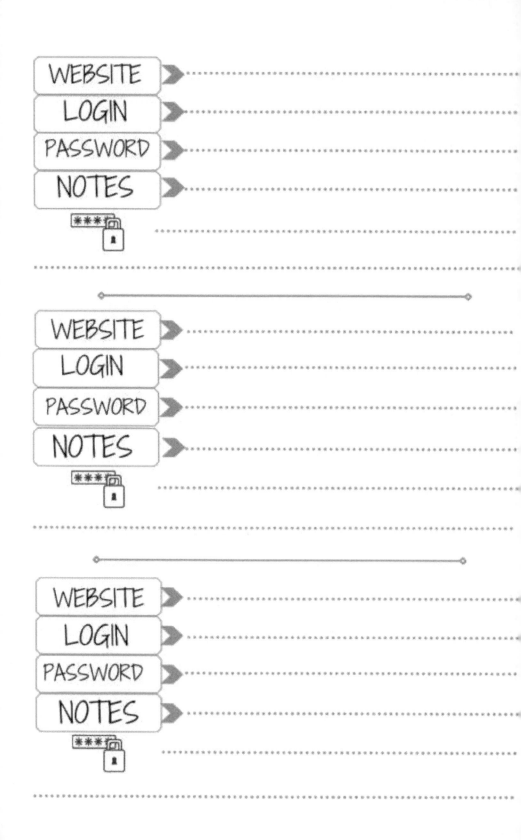

Made in the USA
Columbia, SC
10 August 2023

21488716R10061